Keeping Hope Alive

Keeping Hope Alive

Sermons and Speeches
of Reverend Jesse L. Jackson Sr.

REVEREND JESSE L. JACKSON SR.

Edited by
Grace Ji-Sun Kim

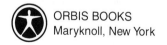
ORBIS BOOKS
Maryknoll, New York

Founded in 1970, Orbis Books endeavors to publish works that enlighten the mind, nourish the spirit, and challenge the conscience. The publishing arm of the Maryknoll Fathers and Brothers, Orbis seeks to explore the global dimensions of the Christian faith and mission, to invite dialogue with diverse cultures and religious traditions, and to serve the cause of reconciliation and peace. The books published reflect the views of their authors and do not represent the official position of the Maryknoll Society. To learn more about Maryknoll and Orbis Books, please visit our website at www.maryknollsociety.org.

Library of Congress Cataloging-in-Publication Data

Names: Jackson, Jesse, 1941- author. | Kim, Grace Ji-Sun, 1969- editor.
Title: Keeping hope alive : sermons and speeches of Rev. Jesse L.
   Jackson, Sr. / Rev. Jesse L. Jackson, Sr., edited by Grace Ji-Sun Kim.
Other titles: Sermons and speeches of Rev. Jesse L. Jackson, Sr.
Description: Maryknoll, NY : Orbis Books, 2020. | Includes
   bibliographical references and index. | Summary: "Selected sermons
   and speeches by Rev. Jesse L. Jackson, Sr., one of the foremost
   champions of civil rights--a moral conscience of this nation"--
   Provided by publisher.
Identifiers: LCCN 2019030819 (print) | LCCN 2019030820 (ebook) |
   ISBN 9781626983595 (paperback) | ISBN 9781608338245 (ebook)
Subjects: LCSH: Jackson, Jesse, 1941---Oratory. | Political oratory--
   United States. | Sermons, American--African American authors. |
   Civil rights--Religious aspects--Christianity. | Social justice--
   Religious aspects--Christianity. | Social change--Religious aspects--
   Christianity. | African Americans--Civil rights. | United States--
   Politics and government--Moral and ethical aspects. | World
   politics--21st century.
Classification: LCC E185.97.J25 J33 2020 (print) | LCC E185.97.J25
   (ebook) | DDC 973.927092--dc23
LC record available at https://lccn.loc.gov/2019030819
LC ebook record available at https://lccn.loc.gov/2019030820

To my mom, Helen, and my grandmother, Tibby

Two young women, whose sense of
selfless sacrifice did not stop with my birth.
They were the source of my moral, ethical foundation;
their missionary vision was inclusive and taught me
the power of selflessness, humility, and courage
and to find joy and fulfillment beyond self-preservation.

Whenever I stray from these principles,
they sit over my shoulder as a guidepost
and a source of conscience.
They taught me the sense of right and wrong,
ethics over ethnicity, a quality of love and justice
that transcends race, color, region, and religion.
They did a difficult thing. They taught me scientific
objectivity, to see others as they are and
not as I would have them to be.

Contents

Speeches 51

Acknowledgments

There are so many people I would like to thank as I put this book together beginning with the many good people at Orbis Books, especially editor-in-chief and publisher of Orbis Books, Robert Ellsberg, who believed in the importance of my work and shepherded me through the editing and production process. I will always be grateful for his patience and kindness in bringing this book to life.

A special thanks is due Dr. Grace Ji-Sun Kim. She had the vision for this book and doggedly pursued it. She encouraged me when I grew weary, demanded that I meet deadlines, and pushed me when I needed it—but always in love. I want to thank Rev. Frank E. Watkins, who helped me in this writing process. He has been with my family and me since 1969. I'm grateful to Rev. Otis Moss Jr. for his steadfast support and long friendship. I will always cherish his very personal Foreword and our struggle together during the long fight for social and economic justice. I also want thank Dr. Eddie S. Glaude Jr. for his very special Afterword. I'm especially pleased and grateful for his keen academic understanding of my activist political theology.

I want to thank many people who have accompanied me on my journey: Dr. Mary Francis Berry; Rev. Andrew Young, whose broad view of the world has been a source of guidance; Rev. Joseph Lowery, a gospel-preaching practitioner of the highest order; Rev. C. T. Vivian, and Rev. Bernard Lafayette, devotees of nonviolence; Rev. James Bevel, a creative genius, whose actions have affected my way of thinking; Diane Nash, who was courage personified for our generation; Rev. Al Sharpton, who gives me credit for giving him guidance, which I certainly hope is justified (I have known him since he was twelve years old, when his mother first brought him to meet me, and I marvel at his growth); Rev. James Lawson, a philosopher, teacher, and fearless practitioner of nonviolence. I am grateful to these persons and so many more, including my jail-mates, James Core, Rev. Al Samson, Rev. Gary Massoni, and Rev. David Wallace, whom I met in seminary, who accompanied me to Selma, Alabama, who helped me expand our Breadbasket and for-mulate my theology. And I would be in error if I didn't give credit to Dr. Obery Hendricks, who has influenced my views on the Jesus of history and mystery. Lastly, I also want to thank Dr. Dwight Hopkins, who helped me in this writing process, and Butch Wing for being part of the movement for several decades.

I also want to thank my family for being there for and with me throughout a life of social and political activism and struggle, beginning with Jacqueline, my wife of fifty-six years, and my five children, Santita, Jesse Jr., Jonathon, Yusef, and Jacqueline Jr. Their constant love and understanding have nourished me throughout our time together in public service and the fight for civil rights. I could not have done it without them.

I especially dedicate this book to all my brothers and sisters who have joined with me in the struggle for peace and justice. Thank you for being by my side as I tried to carry on the dream of Dr. Martin Luther King Jr. and fulfill the assignment he gave me: "Keep hope alive."

Reverend Jesse L. Jackson Sr.

Foreword

I met Rev. Jesse L. Jackson Sr. through two people, the Reverend Dr. Martin Luther King Jr., and my wife, Edwina Moss, who was a member of Dr. King's staff. At that time, I was serving as regional representative of SCLC and the president of Cincinnati (Ohio) chapter of SCLC. It was my privilege to be in the room in 1966 when Dr. King announced the appointment of Rev. Jackson as the Chicago director of Operation Breadbasket. (The following year he was appointed national director.) At the time, Rev. Jackson was a seminary student in Chicago and only twenty-two years old. But from that moment, Rev. Jackson moved to a national stage, which would quickly become a world stage. He has now remained on that global stage of leadership and service for more than a half century.

As one of the founding members of Operation PUSH and the Rainbow PUSH Coalition, I must say it has been a great experience; to witness and share in the unfolding of this gigantic chapter in American history is more than words can convey.

This volume of sermons and speeches is a necessary textbook for youth and adults, both for today and for tomorrow. However, these are only a few chapters of the preaching and teachings of Jesse Jackson Sr. All the workshops, dialogues, Saturday morning meetings, and messages of Rev. Jackson cannot be contained in one volume. His ministry is global. His leadership is a global classroom. If you take a look at the time, places, events, and circumstances where

Rev. Jackson has spoken and preached, these alone will give a profound overview of the height, breadth, and depth of his leadership.

Reverend Jackson's two presidential campaigns, in 1984 and 1988, registered millions of voters and placed scores of women and men in decisive positions that bear fruits of liberation and inclusion at this very hour. But I remember specific events that reflected the measure of the man. I recall in 1983, during the first presidential campaign, when Rev. Jackson called a group of us together and expressed the need for someone to seek the release of Robert Goodman, a Navy lieutenant who had been captured after his plane was shot down over Syria. Rev. Jackson felt that the efforts to get Lt. Goodman released were inadequate and that the longer he remained in the hands of the Syrian government, the more dangerous his situation would become. As the discussion proceeded, there was strong agreement with Rev. Jackson's moral position, but some expressed a dual concern. One, the danger facing Lt. Goodman was imminent. Second, there was the danger facing both Lt. Goodman and Rev. Jackson if Rev. Jackson flew to Damascus to seek Lt. Goodman's release. Reverend Jackson felt the situation was greater than his personal safety or his political future.

He summarized the situation succinctly: "If we seek his release we could fail. If we do not seek his release, we cannot succeed in winning his release. It is better to fail trying to free Lt. Goodman than to face the shame and failure of not even trying." The meeting closed with fervent prayers and profound support to seek Lt. Goodman's release. It ended with Rev. Jackson leading a delegation to Damascus and bringing Lt. Goodman home!

This has been the story of Rev. Jackson's career. I borrow from the late Dr. Vernon Johns: "When the possible is inadequate, experiment with the impossible." This is the theme flowing through Rev. Jackson's ministry and messages: one should not be afraid to experiment with the impossible. This is what the ministry calls us to do. This is what the calling of God places upon our lives.

In the sermons and addresses selected in this book there is a continuing call, a trumpet sound for action—but not chaotic, undisciplined action devoid of moral and spiritual content. The call is for action anchored in love and justice designed for transformational change. Change that empowers the weak, disturbs the powerful, heals the wounded, and liberates the oppressed. This is true whether he is addressing an audience in Soweto, South Africa, or the New Covenant Baptist Church in Orlando, Florida, in Bangkok, Athens, New Delhi, or Saturday morning in Chicago.

In all these talks there is a consistent and powerful message of hope, justice, equality, liberation, equity, human rights, and civil rights. Whether at home or abroad, that theme is expressed with a powerful urgency and consistency. The action called for in these messages is directed at the goal of forming a "more perfect Union" and a more just community, both local and global.

These messages can be a textbook for action and hope for present and future generations.

So many women, men, and children are captured by poverty, racism, sexism, homophobic horrors, and multiple forms of injustice. Great leadership calls us to be courageous enough to experiment with the impossible in order to set free those who are captives or oppressed.

This volume of messages is an open door to a great mansion of many rooms filled with information, gospel truth, challenge, and hope. Far beyond the time of the leader and author of these words, there will be, I believe, a hunger and thirst to know more about him, his era, his service, sacrifices, and courageous contributions against dangerous odds.

Reverend Jackson is an apostle of hope. A disciple of truth. A prophet of liberation.

Reverend Dr. Otis Moss Jr.

Introduction

Grace Ji-Sun Kim

Reverend Jesse Louis Jackson Sr., founder and president of the Rainbow PUSH Coalition, is one of America's foremost civil rights, religious, and political figures. During the past six decades he has played a pivotal role in virtually every movement for empowerment, peace, civil rights, gender equality, and economic and social justice.

Reverend Jackson has been called the "Conscience of the Nation" and "the Great Unifier," challenging America to be inclusive and to establish just and humane priorities for the benefit of all. He is known for bringing people together on common ground across lines of race, culture, class, gender, and belief. On August 9, 2000, President Bill Clinton awarded Rev. Jackson the Presidential Medal of Freedom, the nation's highest civilian honor.

This volume highlights the voice of Rev. Jackson as a preacher and orator—a role in which he has distinguished himself in churches, political conventions, rallies, and universities around the world. The sermons and speeches collected here show how his distinctive commitment to Jesus's liberating message of justice, peace, and equality, addresses the social, political, and economic challenges of contemporary history.

For Jackson, it is difficult to distinguish the function of his speeches and sermons. He views Jesus as God's uniquely gifted son who did not separate the spiritual from the economic and political world. Therefore politics and religion are always intertwined in all his work. Consequently, Rev. Jackson sees himself as "preaching" the gospel when he gives his public speeches and talks.

The six sermons collected in this book are drawn from the small number of surviving sermons. (Most of his sermons and speeches were never written down, and many have been lost.) These few sermons offer the reader a glimpse not only of Rev. Jackson's style of preaching, the dynamic movement of his message, and the power in his delivery, but also the historical contexts, the theological themes, and the engagement with the struggle for social justice that have shaped his life's work.

The contents in this book exemplify the distinct rhythms, beats, tempos, and cadences of African American preaching and oral traditions. One can often hear in them the accented notes, patterns, and movements of black preaching, embodying the hybrid gospel message that intertwines critical political, social, and analytic discourse. Though sermons on the printed page will never capture the energy and power of Rev. Jackson's delivery, they nonetheless enable us to glimpse the strength, motivation, mind, and heart that inspired them.

Jackson has emerged as a principled religious and political leader who is able to analyze the often-hidden workings of an economic system that fails to globalize human rights. His heart for the poor, the outcast, and the forgotten has been emphasized throughout his lifetime of dedication to justice. In all corners of the world his message has made a significant impact on underdeveloped economies and the underutilized minds and talents of the poor. He conveys in his sermons and speeches the message that "everybody is a somebody." Whether living in the slums of Calcutta or New York, those who encounter him have felt his hunger and love to seek justice for all people. Reverend Jackson is a witness to over fifty years of struggle and pain to achieve a fair playing field for all people. This is part of his legacy to our church and our society.

Reverend Jackson comes from the oral tradition of preachers who do not necessarily preach the traditional "three-point sermons" (introduction, three points, and a conclusion). Rather, he preaches his sermons "situationally" out of particular economic and political issues and needs, and structures them as befits the situation. He believes that for the rich the most threatening or challenging biblical verse is the Golden Rule, to "do to others what you would have them do to you" (Matthew 7:12). It is a verse that requires us to do something. And Rev. Jackson adamantly believes that the gospel message is not just a message to be heard or proclaimed but also a message to be lived. It is something that we need to hold in our hearts and then share and live among others.

As I have noted, it is difficult to differentiate between Rev. Jackson's sermons and his speeches. To him, they are both messages of the gospel, just delivered in different contexts. Reverend Jackson's campaign speeches are similar to his sermons. He takes his text from the context and the events of the moment. Similarly, Rev. Jackson's sermons have always been anchored in the events he addressed on a particular day in a particular place.

At times, Rev. Jackson preaches in a conversational manner in order to engage with the listeners. For example, he will query the parishioners and ask them, "How many of you in this church have a relative in jail? How many in this church know someone who is going through home foreclosure? Does anyone know someone who is behind in rent or someone with a student loan debt? Someone who is looking for a job?" Half the congregation will know someone who is in jail. People recognize that student loans become student debt. Thus, much of Rev. Jackson's sermon material is based on the cares and concerns of his audience. These are not lofty thoughts or abstract ideas. They express real flesh-and-blood dilemmas.

Reverend Jackson's preaching draws on the rich traditions of the African American church and the example of many ministers and teachers who have left their mark on his life and work. Among these are Rev. James Hall of Springfield Baptist Church in Greenville, South Carolina, who inspired young Jesse and sent him to his first demonstration. Reverend Jackson's high school football coach, Rev. Joseph Mathis, molded Jackson on the football field, influencing his life off the field and putting him on the trajectory to college. Dr. Samuel DeWitt Proctor, who was Jackson's college president, helped to cultivate his gifts and inclined him to attend seminary rather than law school. Reverend A. Knighten Stanley, who was the campus minister at A & T University, helped Jackson interpret the black people's struggles and understand the time in which he lived. Reverend Otis Moss Jr., who knew Dr. King before Montgomery, was a profound preacher of our time and influenced Rev. Jackson's preaching and the speeches that he gave. Dr. Benjamin Mays, president of Morehouse College, was Jackson's frat brother and helped him through critique and inspiration. Dr. Howard Thurman, a mystic, philosopher, writer, world citizen, with whom Jackson spent countless hours together discussing theology and civil rights, made an impact on his theological journey. His parents' sense of dignity and social justice also shaped Jackson's way of life. All these people were early forces in his life.

The example of Nelson Mandela, the South African freedom fighter, runs through many of these talks. During Mandela's twenty-seven years in prison, he served as a distant source of inspiration. After Mandela's release, the two men met and became friends. As Jackson observed, Mandela was not a churchy person. He didn't talk about God. Rather he lived his beliefs and thereby preached the good news, without calling attention to himself. The struggle against apartheid is one of the themes that runs through many of Rev. Jackson's talks, and later the victorious breakthrough to freedom became one of his touchstones for the power of freedom and justice to overcome oppression. As Dr. King used to say, "The arc of the universe is long, but it bends toward justice." Reverend Jackson would speak at Mandela's funeral, and he continues to invoke his example.

But there is no doubt that the decisive influence for Rev. Jackson came from his encounter with the Rev. Martin Luther King Jr. Jackson spent less time with Dr. King than others who worked closely with him in the South. The Southern Christian Leadership Conference (SCLC) was based in Atlanta, and Jackson's home was in Chicago. However, the speeches and teachings of Dr. King deeply penetrated Rev. Jackson's work, thoughts, aspirations, and visions. He tried to live out Dr. King's work and fulfill the assignment that Dr. King had given him as national director of Operation Breadbasket, and in such a manner continue his legacy.

Many of his talks reference intimate moments with Dr. King, including the stress and doubts he experienced in his last months as he confronted the ongoing war in Vietnam, the falling away of many friends and supporters, and the violence that threatened to erupt from frustrated hopes. As Jackson recalls, King's struggles paralleled the doubts and anguish that Jesus felt as he approached his own passion in Jerusalem. And like Jesus, King somehow found the courage and the faith to go forward.

Dr. King traveled to Memphis, Tennessee, to support a strike by the city's African American sanitation workers. On April 4, 1968, Dr. King was at the Lorraine Motel getting ready to go to supper. He was on the balcony, and Rev. Jesse Jackson was on the street level. Dr. King told Rev. Jackson to put on a tie for supper. Reverend Jackson joked that a "tie wasn't a prerequisite for a meal." At that moment, a shot rang out, and Dr. King fell to the ground, mortally wounded. He died an hour later at St. Joseph's Hospital.

Reverend Jackson has never stopped reminding people of what Dr. King stood for—refusing the urge to replace his radical and prophetic message with a soothing message of "togetherness" that avoids the ongoing sources of conflict. Reverend Jackson reflects that we love martyrs but not marchers. Martyrs are idolized because they can't put pressure on us to act or do anything. Marchers ask us to do something, and many of us don't want to risk or act. We like to idolize and worship, not risk and act. We have to do more than honor Dr. King's memory; we have to follow his example. If we do that, his dream will become a reality.

Reverend Jackson asks two questions: "How do we worship? How do we do justice?" The two are intimately connected. We are called to become peacemakers and not just peacekeepers. Peacekeepers are satisfied with maintaining the status quo. But peacemakers act and seek out that which is broken and needs changing.

People want Santa Claus but not Jesus, because Santa requires nothing from us. People welcome the Easter Bunny but not the cross for the same reason. There is some strangeness in how Christians perceive the crucifixion of Jesus. Reverend Jackson believes "there is a tendency to glorify the cross. If Jesus had died in an electric chair we would be wearing electric chairs around our necks." Too often Christians proudly wear the cross around their necks without understanding the meaning of what they are wearing. They substitute a symbolic cross for the pain, suffering, burden, and meaning of Jesus's actual cross.

Reverend Jackson believes "there are violent policies within our political system, and thus we need to work to help set the captives free. We will all be measured for what we have done. How will Jesus measure us? Jesus will measure us by the way we feed him, clothe him, and visit him in prison."

Jesus was the one who enthroned the oppressed. He shows the way that we can transform society. When Jesus calls us to follow him he means we are to feed or heal or comfort somebody. He calls us to take action. The last night of his life he spent time with Simon the Leper. This is Jesus of Galilee. Jesus is with the marginalized, the poor, and the outcast. And we are to do likewise.

Reverend Jackson looks at his life as a journey of faith. His sermons are not just spoken but embodied in his personal life. When a person's life exemplifies authentic faith, people listen; when such people write, people read; when they walk, people follow them. In fact, we should think about the way we live our lives as being a form of preaching. When Rev. Jackson goes to jail, he is preaching. When he works among poor, disenfranchised, and pained, he is preaching. He doesn't just use words to preach. When we follow that example our lives and lifestyles become our sermons. The "Word became flesh (John 1:14)." Our flesh becomes our words. By our lives we preach. But it can be a struggle to live out a sermon.

Some leaders talk and speak while other leaders reflect. Some lead by the example of their actions. And others, like Rev. Jesse Jackson, not only talk and preach about justice but also embody justice and live it faithfully. He walks the walk of his commitments. Reverend Jackson immersed himself into the global peace and justice and civil rights movements in his college years and has remained an active leader in these and other causes to this moment. His life of service to racial, gender, and economic justice provides a strong example for many to follow, admire, and appreciate. As he has lived out his commitment to civil rights he has also carved out an admirable legacy in American and world history.

Reverend Jackson's sermons and speeches focus on equality, fairness, justice, and civil rights. In both his words and actions he proclaims that all people are equal in God's eyes and all need to be free and have equal rights. He has put his life into a movement of working to make that proclamation a reality. It's a movement to help build the kingdom of God on earth as it is in heaven.

Without hope we will find no reason to continue our work for justice and equality. Hope is the message that comes through in his sermons and speeches. Reverend Jackson proclaims and lives the need to "keep hope alive."

I hope that the selection of a few sermons and speeches will provide some insight into Rev. Jackson's life and theological journey. It has been a long and blessed journey. He has had his share of tremendous joy and sorrow. As he marches along the path of civil rights activism he continues to touch countless lives, move stones that sometimes seem unmovable, helps to clear a path for the marginalized, and fights to create a level playing field for all. For this we owe him a great debt of gratitude.

Biography

Born on October 8, 1941, in Greenville, South Carolina, Jesse Louis Jackson Sr. graduated from local public schools and enrolled in the University of Illinois on a football scholarship. He later transferred to North Carolina A&T State University, where he played quarterback on the football team, became a student leader, active in civil rights, and graduated in 1964. He debated between a career in law or religion and eventually came to Chicago for theological studies at Chicago Theological Seminary. However, in his senior year he deferred his studies to begin working full-time in the civil rights movement with Dr. Martin Luther King Jr. He was ordained on June 30, 1968, by Rev. Clay Evans, completed his work, and received his Master of Divinity degree from Chicago Theological Seminary in 2000.

Reverend Jackson began his activism as a student in the summer of 1960, seeking to desegregate the local public library in Greenville and then as a leader in the sit-in movement. In 1965 he became a full-time organizer for the Southern Christian Leadership Conference (SCLC). He was soon appointed by Dr. Martin Luther King Jr. to direct the Chicago Operation Breadbasket program, followed in August 1967 by his appointment—in what would be Dr. King's last national appointment—as national director of Operation Breadbasket. In December of 1971 Rev. Jackson founded Operation PUSH (People United to Serve Humanity) in Chicago, Illinois. The goals of Operation PUSH were economic empowerment and expanding educational, business, and employment opportunities for the disadvantaged, women, and people of color.

Reverend Jackson was present at the Lorraine Motel on April 4, 1968, when Dr. King was assassinated. The impact of King's work and sacrifice has remained at the forefront of his subsequent work for peace, social justice, economic empowerment of the poor, and human rights. He has conducted that work on the local, national, and international stage, as well as in the political arena.

In 1984 and 1988, he pursued presidential campaigns on the Democratic Party ticket. His 1984 campaign registered over one million new voters, won 3.5 million votes, and helped the Democratic Party regain control of the Senate in 1986. His 1988 campaign registered over two million new voters, won over seven million votes, and helped boost hundreds of local, county, state, and federal elected officials into office. Additionally, he won historic victories, coming in first or second in forty-six out of fifty-six primary contests. His clear progressive agenda and his ability to build an unprecedented multiracial and multireligious coalition inspired millions to join the political process.

In December 1984 Rev. Jackson founded the National Rainbow Coalition, a social justice organization based in Washington, DC, devoted to political empowerment, issue education, and changing public policy. In September of 1996 the political focus of the Rainbow Coalition and the private sector, economic focus of Operation PUSH merged to form the Rainbow PUSH Coalition to continue the work of both organizations and to maximize resources.

On the international stage, Rev. Jackson became a strong leader in the struggle against apartheid in South Africa. On November 2, 1985, Rev. Jackson joined with Oliver Tambo, Bishop Trevor Huddleston, and others at the 120,000-strong demonstration in London's Trafalgar Square to protest apartheid in South Africa and call on the South African government to free Nelson Mandela. He later met with Prime Minister Margaret Thatcher, appealing to her to drop Britain's support for apartheid, and with Pope John Paul II urging him to speak out against apartheid in South Africa.

For his work in human and civil rights, and nonviolent social change, Rev. Jackson has received more than forty honorary doctorate degrees and frequently lectures at major colleges and universities around the world. In October 1997, Rev. Jackson was appointed by President Bill Clinton and Secretary of State Madeleine Albright as the Special Envoy of the President and Secretary of State for the Promotion of Democracy in Africa.

He has continued to be a leading advocate for a variety of public policy issues, including universal health care (he was the first presidential candidate to advocate for such a system), equal administration of justice in all communities, sufficient funding for enforcement of civil rights laws, for adding an individual right-to-vote constitutional amendment (such an explicit right is *not* in the Constitution), and for increased attention to business investment in underserved domestic communities (a theme that the Clinton administration picked up as the "New Markets Initiative").

Reverend Jackson also supports a broad range of policies to improve education, eliminate poverty, and remind everyone that we are a "one-big-tent-America," with room for all and none left in the margins. A current campaign is "Restructure Loans, Don't Foreclose on Homes," tackling today's housing crisis and the economic and political danger of disproportionate income and wealth, which is currently gripping the world.

As a highly respected and trusted world leader, Rev. Jackson has acted many times as an international diplomat in sensitive situations. For example, in 1984 Rev. Jackson secured the release of captured Navy lieutenant Robert Goodman from Syria, and the release of forty-eight Cuban and Cuban-American prisoners in Cuba. He was the first American to bring home citizens of the United Kingdom, France, America, and other countries who were being held as human shields by Saddam Hussein in Kuwait and Iraq in 1990. In 1999 Rev. Jackson negotiated the release of US soldiers held hostage in Kosovo. In August 2000 Rev. Jackson helped negotiate the release of four journalists held in Liberia who were working on a documentary for Britain's Channel 4.

A hallmark of Rev. Jackson's work has been his commitment to youth. He has visited thousands of high schools, colleges, universities, and correctional facilities encouraging excellence, inspiring hope, and challenging young people to study diligently and stay drug free.

Reverend Jackson has also been a consistent and vigorous supporter of the labor movement in the United States and around the world. He is known as someone who has walked more picket lines and spoken at more labor rallies than any other national leader.

A renowned orator and activist, Rev. Jackson has received numerous honors for his work for human and civil rights and nonviolent social change. In 1991, the US Post Office put his likeness on a pictorial postal cancellation, only the second living person to receive such an honor. He was on the Gallup List of the Ten Most Respected Americans for more than a dozen years. He has received the prestigious NAACP Spingarn Medal, in addition to honors from hundreds of grass-roots, civic, and community organizations from coast to coast.

Reverend Jackson married his college sweetheart, Jacqueline Lavinia Brown, on December 31, 1963. They have five children: Santita Jackson, former Congressman Jesse L. Jackson Jr., Jonathan Luther Jackson, Yusef DuBois Jackson Esq., and Jacqueline Lavinia Jackson Jr.

Sermons

Reverend Jackson has been preaching most of his adult life, a period that spans over fifty years as a civil rights leader. He has preached in many venues, including churches, rallies, meetings, and conferences in the United States and around the world. Most of his sermons are preached without a written manuscript. Of those preached from a manuscript, many cannot be found. A mere six sermons are included here. Nevertheless, these rare sermons provide an insight into the theological journey of an African American civil rights leader whose life has largely been defined by moments of preaching.

At its best the church speaks with a moral voice. When Rev. Jackson preaches he wants people not just to sit and listen to the sermon but to act. He wants people to be stirred to become movers and shakers. He wants his listeners to become active peacemakers and bridge builders, architects of democracy and change. He urges his listeners to work toward justice and equality.

1

The Message of Easter

Rainbow PUSH Headquarters
Chicago, Illinois
April 19, 2003

He is not here: for he is risen, as he said. Come, and see the place where the Lord lay. (Matthew 28:6)

Easter: Is it a ritual or real—resurrection or recital?

The dictionary definition of resurrection is to regenerate, resuscitate, revivify, or revive. Resurrection is to bring from death to life. This is precisely the story of the One who walked this earth just over two thousand years ago—who saved sinners and hung out with the homeless, who fought for the fatherless and preached power for the poor. For this, he was crucified, he died, and he was buried. The good news is that the ground couldn't hold him. On the third day, he rose from the dead. It was a real resurrection and not a ritual recital.

Today, on this Saturday morning, at our weekly Rainbow PUSH Coalition[1] meeting, we all look forward to resurrection Sunday. Easter Sunday, in the Christian tradition, is when the power of justice triumphed over the evil of injustice, when the deep darkness of Calvary was shattered with the bright beams of the resurrection hope. Jesus had to suffer and struggle to get to new life. His was serious business, having implications for the life and death of the poor, the workers, the widows, and the sick of his time then and of our time today.

3

We know that during tomorrow's Sunday services throughout the country there will be celebrations and rituals of the drama of Jesus' crucifixion and resurrection. Churchgoers will be sporting their Sunday best—women wearing some of the most striking hats and men boasting some of their finest suits. In fact, for folks who never attend a church or who participate in a worship service very irregularly, they will make it into a church sanctuary at least two times a year, Easter and Christmas. Tomorrow, Sunday stories will be told and testimony will be given about how you were there when they crucified my Lord. Songs will be sung, sermons will be preached, and tears will be shed, for he is risen for you.

But there is fact and there is fiction. When the real Jesus was crucified, Peter denied him, Judas betrayed him, and the disciples hid from him. Is our Easter process in the contemporary context a ritual or is it real? Do we really know about the real pain, abandonment, and suffering endured by Jesus? As the Roman state and the official religious leaders crucified him and committed a crime against the Savior, there were no demonstrations and no political protests. The folks who were the beneficiaries of his miracles were absent. The blind man was not there. Jesus had cured him. The prostitute was not there. Jesus had forgiven her. The five thousand he fed were not visible. Jesus had relieved their hunger. The lame were not there. Jesus had made them to walk. The guests at the wedding—where he turned water into wine—were not there. It is obvious that the people admired him but did not follow him. They accepted the rewards, but they did not engage in the struggle. They celebrated when times were pretty and miracles were present. They left the Savior when pressure and persecution covered the land.

And what about us today? Are we ritual or are we real? Tomorrow it will be easy to wear pretty clothes to the party or to church, but these things will not be required to go to Calvary. To get to resurrection Sunday you have to go through Calvary. Calvary is a real price, not a ritual party. Calvary calls us to put on some work boots when we march to free the wrongfully convicted, when we say no to the bombing of innocent people, when we fight the cutbacks in health care, education, jobs, and environmental protection.

The Easter story is easy reading because the outcome is known. It is easy reading—someone dying for you and rising from the grave like superman. Too many Christian believers seem to treat it like a Hollywood production—the props and blood are not real; the good guy easily gets the woman in the end. But in reality, to save the world from war, pestilence, and famine, Jesus bore the cross alone. If we are to take Jesus's salvation and justice work seriously, then beyond Calvary and beyond the grave is the challenge of the war in Iraq, of people starving in Mississippi, of racism in the church, and of the marketing of religion in a way that does not present the reality of the challenges of suffering, sacrifice, or redemption. The cost of discipleship is, indeed, costly.

There is this story full of drama and danger. In fact, the ancient Hebrew prophet Isaiah, seven hundred years before the birth of Jesus, projected that the Savior would be born to carry out the prophecy of good news for all of humankind. The incarnation of Jesus in the world was filled with drama and danger. Wrought with life-and-death risk, Jesus was born, despite the fact that Herod had put forth a decree throughout the land demanding the violent murder of all firstborn children to prevent the realization of the prophecy. Jesus grew older, and the brilliance of his salvation and justice-making work on earth shone forth. As he performed successful miracles, he faced and overcame the constant spying, taunting, and entrapment of the Sadducees and the Pharisees. Betrayed by one of his disciples, captured and crucified on an old rugged cross, Jesus was the victim of the most historic lynching on a tree. Throughout his ministry he remained faithful despite despicable deeds and a disgusting death carried out by those who conspired against him. Jesus knew he must be a witness to and a servant of God's will, all the while he endured much pain.

Jesus went through three dramatic moods in the final hours. We see him first enduring torment when he retreats to the Garden of Gethsemane, where his mind became troubled and his soul became sorrowful. Second, he knew the pernicious path of Calvary. He understood the physical, bloody pain of nails in his body, and the psychological pain of being put on public display. But he also realized the price of not bearing the cross; all of humanity's and creation's salvation and liberation were at stake. Pain bearing the cross; pain avoiding the cross. In a moment of anguish and torment, he cried out to his Father to "let this cup pass from me." He asked his daddy to remove this awesome weight of suffering. And third, even at that moment of praying to God, and even when Jesus's human side became weakened and weary, he still followed his faith to the end and gasped out, "Nevertheless not as I will, but as thou wilt."[2]

Before Jesus got to hallelujah resurrection, before he got to glorious Easter Sunday, he understood the rocky road to death. And then he could fulfill the prophecy to save the ungrateful. And then he, himself, would be saved by the Father, raised into heaven to sit at his right hand. To ultimately be in good standing with the father, like Jesus, you have to go through some drama and danger.

We all want the resurrection, we all want the new life, and we all want the new hope. But remember what Frederick Douglass said:

> The whole history of the progress of human liberty shows that all concessions yet made to her august claims, have been born of earnest struggle. . . . If there is no struggle there is no progress. Those who profess to favor freedom and yet deprecate agitation are men who want crops without plowing up the ground, they want rain without thunder and lightning, they want the ocean without the awful roar of its many waters. . . . Power concedes nothing without a demand. It never did and it never will.[3]

Only the righteous struggle leads to a righteous life. To get to new life, in Matthew 25, verses 36–46, Jesus gives us the criteria. And those criteria for new hope in good standing with the Father are: did we clothe the naked, did we visit the prisoner, did we tend to the sick, did we welcome the stranger, did we give water to the thirsty, and did we provide shelter to the homeless? Jesus called these folk the least of these. Like him, they were victims of Roman occupation, endured extreme poverty, and were despised by the official temple leadership.

Crucifixion precedes the resurrection. All of this is real, not ritual or play acting. But folks spending all of their money on superficial symbols and clothes to be seen in an Easter festivity are play acting. All of those who sponsor Christmas and Easter parades don't believe in either miracle. They don't have faith in the birth of the Savior, which is Christmas.

Real faith is faith in the real man Jesus who worked this earth. Real faith is faith in the tumultuous circumstances of his birth. Herod had proclaimed a genocidal order to kill all children born male. If found, baby Jesus would have been murdered. His parents, Mary and Joseph, had to hide and disguise themselves, and suffer danger as they secretly escaped to Egypt as refugees—not as forced immigrants looking for a better life for a child, but as political refugees trying to save the life of a child. This is the true story of the birth of the Savior; this is Christmas faith.

The superficial believers don't have faith in the resurrection, which is Easter. Graveyards cannot contain a bloodied body removed from a rugged cross. That is why Easter is a costly redemption. We are redeemed after a sacrificial struggle with principalities and powers. Putting Nelson Mandela in a tomb empowered the struggle for a new South Africa. Killing Martin Luther King Jr. at thirty-nine empowered several generations of freedom fighters. Killing Emmett Till[4] at fourteen empowered the Montgomery bus boycott. Righteous marchers are often resurrected martyrs. This is Easter faith.

Too many of us posture and prance on Easter and Christmas, play-acting faith and reducing it to a ritual, while business institutions are just making money with our willing participation. They are shucking and jiving with our empty celebrations while they laugh all the way to the bank.

Now Palm Sunday was a real drama, Jesus challenging the government. Here was this powerful Roman government, this imperial power, threatened by a man without money, without weapons, who obeyed his father's will perfectly and loved his fellow man unconditionally. Such perfect love casts out fear. And a fearless person is not afraid of loss of jobs or stature or money or death. He becomes dangerous because he is possessed by a countercultural strength.

We worship the cross as a symbol and wear it to show our kinship with Jesus. But Rome had a warehouse full of crosses that they hung people on. It is not the cross but the man on the cross, the causes that he espoused and the people for whom he sacrificed.

The cross was Rome's electric chair. It was no symbol of worship. If Jesus had been lynched in an electric chair, folks would be walking around here today with big old electric chairs for necklaces. You'd see huge electric chairs hanging from walls of the churches. They'd be saying, "It was in the electric chair where I first saw the Lord." It's not form and fashion of ritual. It's the nitty-gritty risk of reality.

It is the man who voluntarily died so we might live, and so fear and death might lose their power. In the end, Jesus was not partying with the rich young ruler or fund-raising with the wealthy in the mansion. His focus was on serving the poor and defending the needy. He was charged with treason, spent a night in jail, and was nailed to a cross like a criminal with wounds in his hands, blood running down his body, and two thieves on crosses beside him. No, he was not with the rich; not partying but enduring pain; the price we pay for justice. The issue remains not the cross, but who was on the cross, and what action got him placed there, and why the priests, the temple leaders, and the government turned on him. The government thought to kill him because the lame, the blind, the weary, and the weak accepted him as the leader of the downtrodden. He moved the people to hope, and the crowd followed him. The powerful sought to crush the spirits of the weak and the vulnerable by killing Jesus physically. The government needs to control the minds of the masses. But Jesus offered them a new way, a way without government taxes, usury, fear, and manipulation. And the religious leaders hated him. He was not a favorite among other preachers. He would not have been their annual revivalist. He opposed the preachers who turned the temple into a treasury for a den of thieves.

Today, Jesus would be killed and rejected because he would choose the mothers of all babies rather than the "mother of all bombs" that were dropped on Iraq.[5] The real question remains today: what would Jesus be doing in light of today's challenges—in the face of the destruction of Babylon by bombs, the military budget versus the education budget, the treatment of women in the marketplace, and racism?

As a risen savior with all power, we who follow him have power to do all things through Christ, for he strengthens us. Tomorrow on Sunday, will we use our strength to dye Easter eggs, wear an Easter bonnet, model new clothes, and get deeper in debt, or will we use our power to set the captives free who have been wrongfully convicted? How many jails will we visit on Easter Sunday, those young and wrongfully convicted men and women? We do know that Jesus was on death row, accused of treason, jailed all night, and finally a victim of capital punishment. Will we use our power to emancipate the enslaved and end racial oppression? Do we use our power to end economic exploitation and stop the war machine? The US military buildup is $400 billion a year and rising. Isaiah admonished us to study war no more and go another way.[6] Take weapons of mass destruction and turn them into creating expanding life options for people.

Jesus promised if you follow him and risk for justice, engage in selfless sacrifice, survive rumors, survive false arrest, survive wrongful conviction, survive death row, survive abandonment by disciples and relatives, and be willing to suffer for the ungrateful, eternal life—resurrection would be the grand prize.

Jesus's way is not convenient; it is uncommon sense, it is countercultural, and it is swimming upstream. The ritual is easier than the reality because it is risk free.

I was in Memphis last Friday, April 4th, as I had been in Memphis April 4, 1968, the day Dr. Martin Luther King Jr. was killed. In 1968, Dr. King led us as we marched to support garbage workers who could not get collective bargaining and against the US war in Vietnam that was tearing the nation apart—that was real.

Now this April 4, 2003, the garbage workers fighting to be recognized were on one side of town. Marchers from LeMoyne-Owens College staged a symbolic march to commemorate the thirty-fifth anniversary of Dr. King's assassination on the other side of town.[7] They were commemorating Dr. King's death in Memphis. Dr. King came to Memphis in 1968 to organize garbage workers and protest the US bombing of Vietnam. But this particular 2003 march, which was a ritual, had little connection to the workers fighting for justice and little connection to the fight against right-to-work laws, and little connection to the opposition against the premise of the bombing of Iraq in March 2003.

The April 1968 march was one of drama and danger. Dr. King assembled his staff at his Atlanta office. It was an unplanned gathering. In fact, I was called Friday, the night before, to catch a plane early Saturday morning. There were about ten of us in his office. And he began to muse in a deep, dark depression:

> Where are we in our struggle? We've won public accommodations. We've won the right to vote. And we're caught up in this ungodly war and unbounded poverty. I've had a migraine headache for the last three days. Maybe I should just quit. Maybe I've done as much as I can in thirteen years. Some of my best friends have turned on me. The press turned on me. Democratic Party allies, they've turned. Maybe I should just go to Morehouse and become president of the college or maybe just write books."

But it seemed that as he talked more and more, he preached his way through and then said: "Let's move forward."

At that time in 1968, I remember watching Dr. King go through these three painful dramatic moods in 1968. After several days of migraine headaches, he said:

1. I thought about turning back. Maybe I've done as much as I can do. Our movement is in disunity now; some differences over philosophy; some differences over strategy.
2. I even considered fasting to the point of death.
3. We should turn a minus into a plus and move on, on to Memphis, move on to Washington, DC, for the Poor People's Campaign.[8]

Dr. King talked himself out of death and said let's move on to Memphis and the nation's capital.

This reminded me greatly of the similar three moods that Jesus went through at the point of his death. Dr. King spoke to us staff folk on Saturday, March 30. That Thursday, April 4th, he was assassinated. Jesus too was beginning to face the gallows. He too mused in a deep, dark depression: "My disciples, they denied me. They're hiding and denying they know me. I pray alone and they sleep. The government is against me. The religious leaders are attacking me. I'm being accused of mixing religion with politics. I've been accused of treason." But somehow, the more he mused, the more he talked and prayed his way out of it. At the end, he said: "God, not my will but your will be done. Let's move forward."

I later reflected that Dr. King's three moods were like those of Jesus before his death:

1. Let this cup pass from me.
2. He agonized and prayed as the disciples slept.
3. Not my will but thy will be done.

The temptation is to look at the lives of Jesus the Christ, Dr. King, and Nelson Mandela and reduce them to ritual. If you go to the tomb in Jerusalem (where Jesus was buried) or you go to the balcony in Memphis (where King was killed) or you go to the prison of Robben Island in South Africa (where Mandela was incarcerated for twenty-seven years), they are not there, the stones have been rolled away.

In the case of Dr. King, a mortal man without guns or wealth, his spirit has been resurrected with such compelling power until no president, no senator, no Supreme Court justice, no billionaire is in the same zone.

In the case of Nelson Mandela, after twenty-seven years in the tomb, he emerged one Sunday morning, freeing his own jailer, taking over the government, and becoming a global moral authority whose name is synonymous with emancipation. That is a lot of stature for an ex-convict. In the case of Jesus, he suffered indignities from the government, a betrayal of his disciples, but trusted God absolutely. Such a trust, such a relationship, was too powerful for the grave to contain; such a power is available to us today.

We too can heal sin-sick nations.

We too can make the lame to walk.

We too can cure diseases, but you got to leave the grave.

Beyond the grave is the resurrection. Beyond the grave are the challenges being fought against poverty, predators, prisons, and for peace. And these are difficult challenges. They invite the scorn of government and frighten friends who will run and hide. But if you hold on to Jesus's hand and to Jesus's formula, you will realize resurrection.

2

The Moral Center

Riverside Church
New York City
March 20, 2005

The prophet Isaiah taught us:

And he shall judge among the nations, and shall rebuke many people: and they shall beat their swords into plowshares, and their spears into pruning hooks: nation shall not lift up sword against nation, neither shall they learn war any more. (Isaiah 2:4)

Dr. Martin Luther King Jr. was not only a dreamer, but he was also a drum major for justice. He was a civil rights leader, an anti-war prophet, a deeply religious man, and an apostle of nonviolent change.

Almost thirty-eight years ago (April 4, 1967), Dr. King stood in this church and called for "a radical revolution of values."[1]

He taught us: "A true revolution of values will soon cause us to question the fairness and justice of many of our past and present policies. . . . A true revolution of values will look uneasily on the glaring contrast of poverty and wealth. . . . A true revolution of values will lay hands on the world order and say of war: 'This way of settling differences is not just.'" In fact, the most dangerous and threatening value to the prevailing order is the Golden Rule: Do unto others as you would have them do unto you (Luke 6:31). Here we find one set of rules and a level playing field. But the

13

games we often play are like breaking the wishbone of the chicken. After the two parts of the bone are broken off, whoever has the largest piece wins over the other player.

After preaching this sermon, one year later to the day, Dr. King was assassinated. The timing has never seemed coincidental. His murder has never been fully resolved. Our movement has never fully recovered. The world has never been fully the same.

Dr. King challenged the American war economy because he knew that the war on poverty would pay the price for the war on foreign countries, as it still does, even today.

Dr. King recognized that politics could be redefined, society turned inside out and upside down, if people—poor people, working people, and especially *young people*—acted on behalf of the *moral center*. The moral center is often seen as radical—radically out of step when two different parties have the same assumptions and eat from the same trough. For example, the *kind* slave master said you've got to control enslaved blacks by giving them a little more to eat. Be kind to them; they can be of value. The *mean* slave master said you've got to treat black people harshly. They are your property; do what you want with them. Kind slave master, mean slave master, but neither one wanted to abolish slavery. The third rail is to abolish slavery. That is the *moral center*. The moral center, the third rail, says end the whole system. Neither kindness nor hostility is the answer. The abolitionist answer, that's the moral center. The moral center is seen as radical because it goes against the grain of the prevailing culture.

In fact, there are three approaches to the moral center. Martin Luther King often use to say: Vanity asks the question: Is it popular? (Everybody wants to be accepted in some measure.) Politics asks the question: Can it win? (An attempt to put square pegs in round holes in order to win.) But morality and conscience ask the question: Is it right? It may be neither popular nor political. The only question is: Is it right?

He reminded us that "the arc of the moral universe is long, but it bends toward justice."[2]

On January 15, 1968, Dr. King spent the day, his last birthday, with his staff. We were making plans for a three-point agenda:

- to pull together a multiracial, multireligious coalition with a commitment to mass action to fight a war on poverty and end the war on the poor;
- to make sure civil rights laws were enforced, not weakened, by the use of race-baiting as a diversion;
- to end the war in Vietnam, choosing containment and negotiation over endless bombing and confrontation, which was robbing our nation of both its innocence and its young.

He came into that meeting a little bit late, as was typical. But he was upbeat. First, he had breakfast with his family that morning at eight o'clock in the morning. Second, around ten o'clock, he came to the church to lead the staff meeting. He was wearing dungarees, a windbreaker jacket, and a sports shirt. He gathered us together to focus on a plan to end poverty and structural inequality. In the room were some Native Americans from an Indian Nation, some African Americans from the Deep South, some Latino Americans from Cesar Chavez's group in the Southwest, and some Jewish allies from New York. And we discussed tactically how to organize a poor people's campaign toward Washington, DC.[3] To DC, some would come by horse, some by mule trains, some by train, some by bus, and some would fly. When we got to Washington, the plan was to set up a Resurrection City, a City of Hope. The tents were already being put up in DC, and Walter Fauntroy was organizing them.[4]

Around noontime, Xernona Clayton and Bernard Lafayette brought in a cake and some punch. We all paused and had a bite of cake and sipped some punch. And then after that short break, we began to plan the afternoon session on how to end the war in Vietnam. So Dr. King spent his own last birthday (a) eating breakfast at home with his family; (b) organizing a plan to end poverty in the basement of a church with his work clothes on, sleeves rolled up; (c) celebrating in a small, measured way with cake and punch;

and (d) laying out a strategy on how to end the US war on Vietnam. That's how he spent his last birthday.

There is a huge gap between Dr. King's birthday today—with the parades and holiday festivities—and the practical commitment Dr. King showed on his last birthday. The King holiday should be the day, the week, to register the most voters, the week to expose the most corporations that don't have fair hiring practices, and the week to expose the most contradictions in local, county, and state budgets relative to fair distribution. Now King celebrations have become disconnected from changing the social order in which we live.

Now we've come full circle. Let us keep our eyes on the prize, on that same three-point agenda. Even today, we must fight a war on poverty, enforce our civil rights and voting rights laws, and give peace a chance by bringing our troops home now from Iraq and Afghanistan.

To carry out that three-point agenda is the right thing to do. It is the moral thing to do. What is right surpasses our narrow political categories. What is right does not bend to the winds of political expediency or to the latest fad in society. It does not waiver before the powers of opposition or the ignorance of the uninformed.

The moral center is not left or right. Abolitionists were not conservatives or liberals; they were the moral center, and eventually they won out.

Civil rights marchers in the South were not backed initially by either liberal or conservative Southerners; but they had right on their side, and ultimately, marching for the moral center brought down the "Cotton Curtain."

Those who opposed the Vietnam War had to struggle against both liberal Democrats and conservative Republicans; but the war was wrong, and finally the moral center became the political mainstream.

Jesus measures the moral center by how we treat "the least of these." By that measure, the George W. Bush budget and the Bush tax cuts miss the moral center. Jesus taught us to feed the hungry;

clothe the naked; shelter the homeless. The president's budget does none of these. Instead, it favors the rich, those who could not conceive of shedding all their possessions to gain entry into heaven. Jesus clearly commands us not to be lured by the stuff of the rich young ruler:

> Jesus said unto him, If thou wilt be perfect, go and sell that thou hast, and give to the poor, and thou shalt have treasure in heaven: and come and follow me. But when the young man heard that saying, he went away sorrowful: for he had great possessions. Then said Jesus unto his disciples, Verily I say unto you, That a rich man shall hardly enter into the kingdom of heaven. And again I say unto you, It is easier for a camel to go through the eye of a needle, than for a rich man to enter into the kingdom of God. (Matthew 19:21–24)

As I reflect on these verses, the rich become too addicted to privileges and being served and laws of inheritance to get humble enough to care for the dispossessed. Jesus didn't say it couldn't happen. He just said it is difficult and unlikely.

This administration's budget is not a moral budget under the rules Jesus laid down; the tax cuts are also not moral. The Bush budget is "mansion down" not "manger up." Tax cuts for the wealthy are top down, and the water does not hit the roots. He expects a blossoming flower to come from dry roots. But those roots are dry for some simple reasons. They were not watered, they were not educated, they were not incentivized, and they were not believed in.

One way to tell the story of America is the story of an expanding democracy attained through struggle. Nonviolent struggle. Coalition struggle. Principled struggle.

The Sons of Liberty threw tea into Boston Harbor. The abolitionists, Henry David Thoreau, Abraham Lincoln, Walt Whitman, and Frederick Douglass fought against slavery, war, and poverty. The women of the suffrage movement chained themselves to the White House fence. "Bread and Roses" occurred, and United

Auto Workers' sit-down strikes happened in Flint, Michigan. There were also Cesar Chavez's grape and lettuce boycotts, and the Montgomery bus boycott. There was a march on Selma and a letter from a Birmingham jail. There was Seneca and Stonewall and also Dr. King and the March on Washington. There were the Freedom Riders and Freedom Summer. There was the Port Huron Statement, the Vietnam Moratorium, and the hunger strikes and sit-ins against apartheid. There was a nuclear freeze rally in Central Park, and on February 15th, 2003—the world said no to war. There is a fight for the right to vote and the right to have every vote count.[5]

We meet here today as part of that tradition and part of that struggle. We are at a low point, but we have been down before. We should not feel guilty for being down; but it is up to us to get back up. As Muhammad Ali told us, "The ground is no place for a champion."[6] And the darkest hour is always just before the dawn.

I do not agree with the current administration/media spin that the fact of the recent Iraqi elections and the bravery of the Iraqi voters now means that our attack on Iraq was justified.

First of all, in the immortal words of Zhou Enlai about the French Revolution, "It's too early to tell."[7]

More fundamentally, the immorality of a preemptive strike is not altered by its apparent success. Your senior minister, James A. Forbes, said this was an immoral war before it ever started. The pope said that this was an unjust war. The archbishop of Canterbury opposed this war. The leaders of almost every major religion across the globe said that a preemptive strike was immoral.

Nelson Mandela, the greatest moral voice of recent times, spoke out strongly against a unilateral, aggressive, preemptive strike. President Bush's preemptive strike was wrong. It was morally wrong and wrong under international law. It was wrong under his own religious beliefs—whether or not he now believes it turned out successfully despite the lies he used to get our nation into it.

Our country will have to live with the future consequences of this strike—not just next week but for the next several decades. Our moral authority in the world has been weakened. So when

China rattles its sabers at Taiwan what can we say about it? Do we say that preemptive strikes are only good for America?

President Bush launched us on a new course, a foreign policy of preemptive war that marks a radical departure from prevailing international law, human rights, the right of self-determination, and economic justice as a fair policy. His new policy was never seriously debated in Congress; the public never vetted it; it was never offered to the voters as a choice in a campaign, which is essential in a democratic system.

Clearly, the voters never gave their consent to the Bush Doctrine of preemptive war. This was an Iraq war based on lies. Iraq had no weapons of mass destruction. Yet those who assisted with those lies have been promoted.

This was a war that violated the Ten Commandments. You shall not kill. Neither shall you steal. Neither shall you bear false witness against your neighbor.

Neither shall you covet your neighbor's oil fields.

The American government deceived the American people into the war. The rest of the world understands that, even if many Americans still do not. How misleading was this Bush war. We lost lives, money, and honor. How President Bush used September 11, 2001, as a pretense to strike. When he was later asked to apologize for his war of invasion, his answer was "that was just the way I felt," or some similar simple-minded comment.

United States presidents operate this way because we do not accept membership in the World Court. We hold other nations to World Court standards, but we will not abide by the standards ourselves. Basically, our foreign policy is above the law—without accountability and transparency; it's undemocratic; it's above the law. Absolute power corrupts absolutely.[8] Ultimately, the ancient axiom holds true: the arrogance and pride of a nation precede the fall of a nation.

At least 100,000 Iraqis have died; some estimates have it higher. Fallujah is decimated. Weapons of mass destruction were never found in Iraq, but our nation may have used them. Our army has tortured. Our government lawyers have condoned torture. Our president promoted an apologist for torture to attorney general, and most of our legislators voted okay. Our stature in the world is as low as it has ever been.

Once again, the Bush administration has chosen the lonely road. And unlike the Good Samaritan, they are abandoning the Jericho traveler in the ditch.[9]

This evening, we pray for peace. We gather our strength for the long struggles ahead. We light a candle. We reflect on life and death, and the value of a young child. And in the deepest traditions of American dissent and patriotism, traditions running back to Thomas Paine and Thomas Jefferson, to Frederick Douglass and Sojourner Truth, to Cesar Chavez and Delores Huerta, to Martin Luther King and Robert Kennedy, we do object to this war.[10]

Someday soon, swords will be beaten into plowshares.

Someday soon, lions will lie down with lambs. How strange they might appear to be. What do they both have in common? Neither wants to feel acid rain on their backs or the forest to catch on fire.

Someday soon, justice will roll down like waters and righteousness like a mighty stream.

> If my people, who are called by my name, will humble themselves and pray, and seek my face and turn from their wicked ways, then I will hear from heaven, and I will forgive their sin and will heal their land. (2 Chronicles 7:14, NIV)

We need healing and hope. And the moral center will get us there.

3

Beauty from the Ashes

Regina Mundi Church
Soweto, South Africa
June 18, 2006

Arise; shine, for thy light has come, for the glory of the Lord has risen up for thee. For, behold, the darkness shall cover the earth, and gross darkness the people; but the Lord shall arise upon thee; and his glory shall be seen upon thee. (Isaiah 60:1–2)

The spirit of the Lord God is upon me; because the Lord hath anointed me to preach good tidings unto the meek, he hath sent me to bind up the broken-hearted, to proclaim liberty to the captives, and the opening of the prisons to them that are bound. (Isaiah 61:1)

To grant those who mourn [in] Zion, giving them a garland instead of ashes, the oil of gladness instead of mourning, the mantle of praise instead of a spirit of fainting. So they will be called oaks of righteousness, the planting of the Lord, that he may be glorified. (Isaiah 61:3)

This, then—beauty from ashes, light from darkness, hope from despair, victory when there is seemingly certain defeat—written centuries ago, remains our hope for today. All around we see evidence of the need to replace ashes with beauty, destruction with reconstruction, and collapse with rehabilitation.

21

In Luke 4:18–20, we hear Jesus the Rabbi quoting Isaiah in the temple, many years later, saying the same thing.

> The Spirit of the Lord is upon me, because he has anointed me to bring good news to the poor. He has sent me to proclaim release to the captives and recovery of sight to the blind. To let the oppressed go free. To proclaim the year of the Lord's favor. And he rolled up the scroll, gave it back to the attendant, and sat down. The eyes of all in the synagogue were fixed on him. (NRSV)

We hear from Isaiah and from Jesus the message of justice and the purpose of the Savior. When the infinite met the finite, Jesus was born. Not in a high-class mansion but in a low-lying manger did he come. God incarnated Godself into a man with a plan for the meek and the mournful. The Gospel of Luke is clear. Jesus walked on this earth with one mind and one mission: to allow the oppressed to go free. If the church is to be faithful to the One for whom the church is a witness, then Jesus's mission statement is the mission statement of the church. Cultures change. People change. Situations change. And the times, they are a-changing. But the mission persists forever. That is the good news. There is an enduring message that falls afresh on every generation.

And South Africa is a testament of hope to this message and mission. Apartheid came to power in 1948 as the official nationwide policy of South Africa. In fact, the 1948 Afrikaner government borrowed the policy of apartheid from the same practice in the white Dutch Reformed Church of South Africa: a radical white Christianity poisoned with racist assumptions; a radical perversion of the gospel. They also got this policy from the 1896 apartheid decision in America rendered by the US Supreme Court in its *Plessy v. Ferguson* judgment.[1] On June 7, 1892, Homer Plessy, a thirty-year-old black man, a New Orleans shoemaker, was imprisoned for sitting in the whites-only car section of the East Louisiana Railroad. Plessy could have passed for a white man because his skin color was just as light as white people. But he consciously identified as a black man to challenge the Louisiana Separate Car Act. The US Supreme Court supported segregation when it proclaimed that separation between black and white citizens is lawful as long as the conditions of that separation were equal; and so we get the famous separate-but-equal justification for American apartheid. Slavery kicked out in 1863; Supreme Court brings in apartheid in 1896.

From their own white Dutch Reformed Church and the US Supreme Court, the Afrikaner government implemented apartheid. But an apartheid church is a serious attack on the gospel of Jesus. Somewhere or another, they ignored the essence of the story of Jesus and the Good Samaritan, which calls us to move beyond race defining one's authenticity. In the Good Samaritan story (Luke 10:25–37), a man was beaten and robbed. A rabbi of his own religion, he walked by; a Levite of his own ethnic kin, he walked by. Both walked on the other side of the street to distance themselves from the victim. But the Samaritan—a man from another country, another race, who worshiped God differently—stopped to pick him up, put him on his horse, and sent him to get medical attention until his recovery. When Jesus tells this parable, he then asks "Who is your neighbor?" Is it the guy from your own religion, your own ethnic group, or is it whoever comes? Is it kin, character, or race? So these segregated religions are radically disconnected from Jesus's message about caring and character, not race, ultimately determining one's stature.

Here in the apartheid church, members used the Bible to justify taking Africans' water, air, and sacred ancestral lands. Here, in the apartheid church, clergy justified oppression of Africans by preaching that Africans were the heirs of the curse of Ham (Genesis 9). Here in the apartheid church, the military prayed for God's strength before they went out and murdered innocent Africans who were protesting being forced to carry identity papers in their own land.[2]

But yesterday's racist apartheid South Africa was the ashes; today's free and growing democratic South Africa is the beauty.

Now the new South Africa is building the rainbow nation of blacks, "coloureds,"[3] Indians, English-speaking whites, Afrikaner-speaking whites, men, women, Christians, Jews, African Traditional Religions—all are precious in God's sight. You have accepted all eleven languages of your people. The design of your flag symbolizes the unity of your different people. The colors of your flag stand for Africans, English speakers, and Afrikaners. You show us not retributive justice, but truth and reconciliation justice. It is the spirit of *Ubuntu*—I am because of the community. The spirit that says we are all our brothers' and sisters' keepers. South Africa is a metaphor for transformation, healing, and justice. Against the odds, there is always the possibility of hope around the world.

Because you have had this marvelous transformation from ashes to beauty, because your scars have been turned into stars, you are now qualified to lead the world. You are the global community whose beauty out-distances your ashes, and thus you are credible as a people, with a moral authority that is heard around the world.

I first came to Regina Mundi in 1979. I was able to get into South Africa with the support of Oliver Tambo and Johnny Makatini (African National Congress leaders), Jack Odell, and Dr. Howard Schomer (from the US National Council of Churches and former president of Chicago Theological Seminary). And I was a guest of the South African Council of Churches for seventeen days. I visited Crossroads.[4] I saw the hurt and the neglect, which was a metaphor for South Africa in that troubled season. I saw the ashes.

The media was an awesome propaganda arm to justify and rationalize this system.[5]

The fact that I had been allowed entry was a source of controversy in the media before I even entered the country. So when I arrived at the airport, there was a huge number of media that met our plane. They were asking sharp questions as to why I was here, and how I had been allowed in. I said I was in South Africa to study the situation, as a guest of the Council of Churches. I wanted to visit the country and meet with labor leaders and friends. They asked, Why are you really here? Are you going to speak to the political conditions?

I said I want to get a firsthand view of the situation. It was clear to me that South Africa and South Carolina, the state of my birth, were extensions of the same system, driven by the same ideology. And so I thought to avoid confrontation and any confusion at the airport I would say something mild: "I believe in human rights for all human beings. We should measure human rights by one yardstick." I thought that was clear and yet nonthreatening. But it was considered extremely radical, because such a statement was antithetical to the apartheid system.

The very next day there were banner headlines all over the country that I had come to interfere with the system, imposing my values and views. It was apparent that it would be quite a journey across the country and we would meet stiff resistance all throughout this land.

I witnessed the suffering, the intimidation, the police and armed vehicles, the ever-present fear, the grieving widows and children of martyrs. I saw the ashes. But through all of that there was a sense that help was on the way and hope was in the air. The wind of beauty would one day blow in South Africa. Where hate and fear abounded, love and hope abounded more.

I saw school children at the Crossroads Township, the school books that were old and few. I saw teachers with a board attached to a tree, teaching children the alphabet and about their culture. I saw them singing and dancing in the mud, the people in the ashes who refused to hang their harps upon the willows and weep as if they were in some ancient Babylon with no way out.

The spirit of the will to freedom could not be contained by alliances with superpowers, by nuclear weapons hidden in the hills, by jet planes. The spirit could not be contained by lies or be held captive in jails or by crippling poverty. The spirit of the innocent buried in the graves of Soweto[6] thirty years ago cried out, and they would never rest until there was justice for all of God's people in the land.

The songs of the people, the struggle of the people, the hope of the people . . . And the spirit of the living God was in this place, and it was infectious. That is Crossroads. That is Soweto.

I saw the tragedy of racist apartheid South Africa. I attempted to uncover the treasure—the tragedy attempted to cover the treasure, the tragedy of fear, and hatred and violence. The treasure of the soil, and resources and gifts of the poor were being turned to ashes and sent into exile or jailed. But I saw the dream makers defy odds, like a giant phoenix, determined to rise from the ashes.

South Africa, endowed with gold and diamonds and arable land and one of the world's great trade routes, located strategically where the Indian and Atlantic Oceans kissed, connecting the world with access to growth and prosperity.

And yet out of the ashes of this subjugation, a metaphor for the worst of the human spirit, your democracy, led by the likes of Nelson Mandela, Oliver Tambo, and Thabo Mbeki, is now the example for the world.

I was also in Cape Town that glorious Sunday after preaching in Allan Boesak's church,[7] and Mr. Mandela came walking out of jail after twenty-seven years. His release that morning was like a giant hurricane of beauty blowing away ashes. The public had not been allowed to see his face for twenty-seven years. All those years, in the salt mines, in human degradation, we hardly knew what to expect. Perhaps an old man bent over with a stick, hurt by the years of turmoil with thick-rimmed glasses and walking with a cane, perhaps incoherent.

But no, he came out walking upright, strong, sharp mind, with a moral clarity and authority that shook the world. The suffering strengthened his character and his resolve for dignity for himself and for his nation; he had been healed by his stripes; he spoke truth to power like no other.

Beauty was blowing away ashes!

By 1990 that legal system of racist apartheid went down.

But though there is a new birth, there is always after-birth matter; there is always unfinished business. Those countries, corporations, and communities that boycotted the colonial apartheid system that controlled the land are called now to pursue a new agenda: the unfinished business of inadequate education and life-threatening health conditions. There is a need to make up for lost time because of the years of suffering under apartheid. People of South Africa are now free but not equal. Gross disparities between the very wealthy and the very poor have become just as much of a threat as the racial separation was for so many years.

The forces that divested then must reinvest now. Not boycott, but build up. There is a new and better South Africa that has a brighter future than the old and broken South Africa of ashes. But we also know there are those that invested in the old apartheid South Africa that will *not* reinvest in the new democratic free South Africa. Today there are new ashes. There are new ashes in South Africa, throughout the continent, and around the world.

There are the ashes of the genocide in Darfur and the ashes of the killer disease of HIV/AIDS. Five-and-one-half-million people with HIV/AIDS; 25 million in the world died since 1981. Worldwide there are 40.5 million living today with HIV/AIDS, five million new cases each year.

There are new ashes of pain. Political apartheid oppressed and suppressed; today HIV/AIDS kills, governments are bankrupt, and families are destroyed. This is a killer disease; we have the power and ability to kill it before it kills us. We must (a) reduce high-risk behavior; (b) expand education; (c) research for the cure; and (d) provide help for the sick with affordable medicine because it is both morally right and cost efficient.

There are new ashes. The war on poverty must be fought with resources and not just with rhetoric. The need for drinkable water and housing must be met; the war on illiteracy must be fought. There is a need for training in computer skills and trade skills.

Africa deserves a Marshall Plan, a development bank that provides long-term, low-interest loans, and mutually beneficial trade.

As the continent that has subsidized European and US development,[8] Africa is the creditor, not the debtor. In practical terms a well-healed literate and productive continent is of more value than one that is sick and struggling. After World War II the Marshall Plan included fifty-year loans at 2 percent government-secured interest and the home of NATO for defense. This served Europe, the United States, and the world well. Its success should be repeated in Africa.

There is a need to close the gap between the North and its surpluses and the South and its deficits. The South lives in ever-expanding deprivation. Today the extremes of wealth and poverty are threatening to tear us apart at the seams. We have globalized capital but not globalized education, human rights, labor rights, children's rights, and women's rights—or calculated the dangers of global warming.

President Bush's war on terror is illegitimate, and his war in Iraq is misguided. There are those who think it's the right war with the wrong strategy. But it's the wrong war, an unnecessary war with a failed strategy.

It is spreading terror and anger and hatred and fear. It was built on false information like a house built on sand.

We listened to greedy and corrupt informants who whispered false tales to government officials with ears itching for any justification for war. These misguided leaders are more and more isolated. They are the ones who sought to diminish the role of UN observers sent to Iraq to see if that country had offensive weapons. They are the ones who sought to discredit and belittle the overall policy and practice of the United Nations toward the Iraqi crisis. But in Iraq the world discovered that there were no weapons of mass destruction, no al-Qaeda connection, and no imminent threat. Now we are losing young lives, forfeiting their honor, and wasting much money.

The budget for that war, driven by guided missiles and misguided leadership, could have wiped out poverty and made the world a safer and more secure place.

But South Africa teaches the world the other alternative. The beauty of the new South Africa having overcome the piles of ashes and deprivation shows that when there is lots of darkness a little light has the power to dispel it.

You have witnessed to the world how to get beauty from the ashes, and your quest for justice and equality must continue. To fight poverty, to educate every person, to make high-tech computers accessible to everyone—to all this and more you have proven the power of the mission that is greater than the missiles.

You defeated colonialism and apartheid. In this stage you must struggle for access to capital, industry, technology, and reconstruction.

Don't give up now. You must lift the people out of economic despair. Level the playing field of knowledge. Democratize the use of technology.

Through it all and against all the odds, you have proven how the mission described in Isaiah and echoed by Jesus is greater than the missiles. Maintain that mission. Defend the poor and deliver the needy and study war no more.

Maintain that mission. The anointed of the Lord must preach good news to the poor. Proclaim freedom to the captives. Recover sight to the blind. Maintain that moral center which is the high road of moral leadership. It's good for the healing of all nations.

Somehow through the muck and mire of lies and distorted reality and violence, truth marches on. Hold fast to the moral center. Don't let the trade winds of expedient politics alter your sail. You have illuminated the power of the Scripture. You have shown the world by example. You have turned tragedy to treasure. You have turned tyranny to democracy. You have turned jail cells into museums.

You've chosen coexistence over co-annihilation; you've turned ashes to beauty. You have survived the long night of desperate oppression. It's dark, but it's not twilight moving toward midnight. It is midnight moving toward daylight. You survived midnight. Now it is twilight, the dawn of a new day.

Somehow there is evidence that your morning and beauty are within reach. Hold fast to the light. The Lord is our light and our salvation. Through your tears hold fast. Weeping may endure for a night, but joy cometh in the morning. The writer in Chronicles was right when he put forth the formula for healing.

> If my people who are called by my name, humble themselves, and pray, and seek my face, and turn from their wicked ways, then I will forgive their sins, and they will hear from heaven and I will heal their land. (2 Chronicles 7:14)

Keep healing. Keep hoping. Light the whole world from the radiance of your light.

4

Faith without Works Is Dead

**November 2008
(occasion unknown)**

*What good is it my brothers and sisters if you say you have faith
but do not have works? Can faith save you? If a brother or sister
is naked and lacks daily food, and one of you says to them, "Go
in peace; keep warm and eat your fill," and yet you do not supply
their bodily needs, what is the good of that? So faith by itself, if
it has no works, is dead.* (James 2:14–17 NRSV)

My faith tradition has always been inextricably bound with the
tradition of the abolition of slavery, the struggles to end colonial
occupation, and the civil rights movements. The blood, sweat, and
tears of "the movement" have run through my life; they touched
and entangled me with an indelible spirit of never giving up, always
trying to serve. Through the good and hard times, I have leaned on
my faith to help me traverse the twists and turns of life.

I grew up in Greenville, South Carolina, with two strong parents who believed in the literal sense and spirit of the Bible that
required and mandated prayer in all circumstances. They prayed
daily and instilled that belief in me. My parents had a pietistic view
of the faith, with private values and personal dignity. They did
not attach it to social justice and emancipation. Be a good person
and do the right thing—a pietistic faith. Personal dignity meant,

don't violate the person. They were faithful to our local church. My parents participated in all aspects of the church work including tithing, which enabled us to build what we could with what we have and God's help. I learned very early in life that "with God all things are possible."

As I navigated through the South as a youth, and in particular as a college student, I was thrust into the civil rights movement. Racism was alive and well in the segregated South and present in every facet of our lives. It was a "dual society." That operated on two levels. First, socially: blacks could not sit at the same lunch counters as whites; blacks sat at the back of the bus. Blacks were denied equal access to public accommodations. That duality was also economic, with African Americans having little, if any, direct participation in the financial life of the nation.

Seeing the inequities of segregation in all aspects of our lives greatly challenged me to seek another way—a better way. I learned through the teaching of Dr. Martin Luther King Jr. and his contemporary Dr. Leon Sullivan[1] that our plight as people was like that of a symphony. Dr. King's focus was on fundamentally changing the laws to ensure equal protection. Dr. Sullivan stressed the use of the dollar to change within the system. Both were friends, and their efforts were complementary. Dr. Sullivan worked with Philadelphia preachers to use their economic strength to boycott Wonder Bread and other corporations and to demand more black truck drivers and jobs for black people. When they told him that there were not enough blacks trained to do the jobs, he took an old closed-down jail in central Philadelphia and started Opportunities Industrialization Center. He was emphasizing making the system work from within. He brought that program to Dr. King, and Operation Breadbasket grew out of that. The two men were not competing but cooperating.[2] The political and the economic struggle are the different threads in the same quilt, different streams in the same river.

I came to conceptualize our cause and termed it the "Freedom Symphony"—our freedom song for democratic and economic empowerment.

Symphonies are constructed in four movements. The first movement was the fight to end slavery (1619–1865)—a tumultuous upheaval battling the dehumanization of Africans and African Americans. Slavery fueled the global trade markets and the industrialization of America. It was an economic system that confined blacks to "work without wages" and involved total subjugation to the master.

The second movement was our quest to dismantle Jim Crow (1865–1965) and tear down ancient walls of legal segregation that prevented equal, democratic participation in America's social, political, and economic life. But the legacy of decades of slavery and Jim Crow segregation left blacks in a state of inequality. Economic inequalities—two Americas—remained a fact of life. The ultimate tragedy of Jim Crow segregation was not noticeable physical pain, but you learned to segregate your dreams, segregate your aspirations, and segregate your hopes. It was not the pain of segregation; it was the limitations of segregation that were ultimately so destructive. And when there is a wall between two people—plant two seeds of equal strength on each side of that wall. You water them both and put a wall between them. One grows tall and full of fruit. One is stunted. The taller one is not a better one. The shorter one is not a lesser one. The one that had sunshine and photosynthesis grows taller. When the walls come down, we all can grow to our maximum potential together. Thus the growth of the New South. The civil rights movement brought down the legal walls of segregation between black and white.

The third movement was our fight for the right to vote—to open the voting process to all African Americans as well as create and institute new legislation such as the 1965 Voting Rights Act to ensure and protect the rights of all voters.[3] The promise of 1870, the Fifteenth Amendment to the US Constitution, gave African American men the right to vote. But the implementation of that amendment was left in the hands of the Confederates, the former slave owners. They fought a war to deny both our humanity and our right to vote. But slave masters lost the Civil War, and black people were free. Emancipation came, and black people got the right to vote. But then Reconstruction ended; Confederates came back into power. Black people were prevented from voting and Confederates established legal segregation.[4]

The states' rights doctrine of Southern segregationists, for ninety-five years, frustrated the right to vote. For them, states had the right to go against the federal government and the US Constitution. But the frustration was not just for blacks. White women couldn't serve on juries. Eighteen-year-olds couldn't vote but could serve in the Vietnam War. Students couldn't vote on college campuses. Citizens couldn't vote bilingually. And at national political party conventions, candidates could not have delegates proportionate to their popular vote. When the civil rights movement forced all these laws and walls of segregation to come down, it opened all these doors of opportunity, including the opportunity that helped Barack Obama to become elected president.

For example, in 1984 when I first ran for president, I received something like 3.5 million popular votes but only four hundred delegates at the Democratic National Party Convention. At that time, the party had a winner-take-all policy, which meant if I got 49 percent of the vote and you got 51 percent, you took all of the delegates. We had the rules changed to proportionality, so if I got 40 percent of the popular vote, I get that proportion of the delegates. We democratized democracy and the Democratic Party. That party policy change was not appreciated at that time. Then when Barack Obama ran against Hilary Clinton, under the old system, she would have been the winner. She won the big states of California, Texas, Ohio, Pennsylvania, and New York and would have won *all* of those delegates. But once we had democratized democracy, Obama followed the new policy in which he retained all of his delegates proportionately even when he didn't win the whole state. And that was a major key to his victory.

The fourth movement of our Freedom Symphony represents the unfinished business of our struggle—we are free but not equal. Our fight for economic justice, access to capital, industry, technology, and deal-flowing relationships remains at the forefront of today's agenda. Oftentimes, whites can get money and good access to credit based on an idea when blacks can get it only based on collateral. Or when we survey the nation's cities, African Americans own no downtown skyscraper in America.

This fourth movement is one that I believe will take us beyond the margins so that all can participate in the prosperity of our nation. My last days with Dr. King and Dr. Sullivan were filled with watching them motivate and move our nation toward "a more perfect Union." We must be guided by their faith and spurred to social action to ensure that we have equal access to capital, unfettered economic development in urban communities, and fair and equitable professional financial services, which includes deal flow and fee structure.

My faith inspires me to continue to do this work. But faith without works is dead. And so we tackle today's financial calamity[5]—one that now finds us grappling with an ever-spiraling cycle of unemployment, home foreclosures, and rising student loan debt. It is here where faith and works meet. And it is on this philosophy that I seek to serve my God and our world.

5

Wrestling with the Living Word

New Covenant Baptist Church
Orlando, Florida
February 1, 2012

And when he was entered into a ship, his disciples followed him. And, behold, there arose a great tempest in the sea, insomuch that the ship was covered with the waves: but he was asleep. And his disciples came to him, and awoke him, saying, Lord, save us: we perish. And he saith unto them, Why are ye fearful, O ye of little faith? Then he arose, and rebuked the winds and the sea; and there was a great calm. But the men marveled, saying, What manner of man is this, that even the winds and the sea obey him! (Matthew 8:23–27)

Hearken; Behold, there went out a sower to sow: And it came to pass, as he sowed, some fell by the way side, and the fowls of the air came and devoured it up. And some fell on stony ground, where it had not much earth; and immediately it sprang up, because it had no depth of earth: But when the sun was up, it was scorched; and because it had no root, it withered away. And some fell among thorns, and the thorns grew up, and choked it, and it yielded no fruit. And other fell on good ground, and did yield fruit that sprang up and increased; and brought forth, some thirty, and some sixty, and some an hundred. And he said unto them, He that hath ears to hear, let him hear. (Mark 4:44)

For we wrestle not against flesh and blood, but against princi-palities, against powers, against the rulers of the darkness of this world, against spiritual wickedness in high places. (Ephesians 6:12)

I am honored to be a part of this celebration of twenty years of service of the Rev. Randolph Bracy Jr.[1] Two decades is a long time to do anything. It is even more challenging to stay faithful to one's calling in a time of crisis. Often when the waters of life experience are in turmoil, too many waver with weak weather nerves, while others sow seeds of commitment and service and bear fruits of faith. But that is how the best separate from the rest. The tough get going when the going gets tough.

We all know that right now we face a deep crisis. It's not just the statistics of professors and politicians. It is the real life challenges that we face every day. Folks are wondering how they're going to get by.

Let me ask you a few basic questions:

If you have a relative in jail, stand up.

Do you know someone in home foreclosure or behind in their rent? Stand up.

Do you know someone with a student loan debt? Stand up.

Do you know someone with a credit card debt? Stand up.

Do you know someone searching for a job? Stand up.

Do you know someone who has considered suicide? Stand up.

Now, the overwhelming number of you stood up because no one in America is immune, removed, or untouched by this all-per-vasive crisis. It is a crisis that impacts all of us but most especially the poor, the bruised, and the left out.

But crisis breeds opportunity. Opportunity produces leaders. Leaders speak truth to power. Prophets struggle with principalities and powers in high places.

Today we need the prophetic voice of Randolph Bracy Jr., who embodies the living word. I congratulate you on being a long distance runner. As we know, many start fast but don't last. Or they plant seeds in sand, and those seeds don't germinate. Or their seed is not planted deep enough and is blown away by the wind. Reverend Bracy, your seeds germinated and bore fruit. As a matter of fact, you didn't just grow a flower or a tree, you built a garden; you built an orchard. You didn't build a church building, which can be taken away by a hurricane or a fire. You built a community of faithful, knowledgeable believers. You built a church that is deeply rooted in sound theology and sociology, rooted in commitment to education, inspiration, and social justice.

In twenty years, the race does not go to the swift or to the strong but to those who endure, those who hold out, those who last. New Covenant Baptist Church in Orlando is a frame of reference for those around the country. Some megachurches have small messages. Your church has a megamessage.

As Jesus fed the multitude, he showed what it means to have no church building but a megaministry. Jesus fed people wherever they were without regard to status. Theologically you apply the Bible to people's circumstances and not just apply the people to the biblical circumstances. This keeps you current, and it is called the living word. American sermons, unfortunately, for the most part, are not connected to the reality of our political circumstance. That's the other entrapment of pietism without social philosophy. Here folks are in Babylon, but preachers refuse to preach against Babylonian captivity. Here folks are in Egypt, but preachers refuse to preach against Egyptian slavery. Here folks are in segregation, but preachers preach in a comfort zone rather than about liberation.

In contrast, Rev. Bracy has applied a good mind to challenging circumstances. Throughout the urban areas of Florida and the whole nation, people are hurting and seeking healing from a war on the poor and not a war on poverty. We have to be clear. Some of our areas are suffering as if it were the aftermath of a war. These are challenging circumstances.

Witness the sense of abandoned houses. Banks used subprime and predatory lending to target, steer, and cluster black and brown families to take away their homes and drive them into poverty. Banks gave misleading and faulty mortgage loans to the vulnerable. When the vulnerable couldn't meet their unjust mortgage notes, banks took the people's homes away. And all of these banks were found guilty; they went to the federal government and worked out a settlement, which they paid. But not one bank has been charged with a crime. And most of the money paid went back to the government treasury and was not used to reconstruct the houses that the banks repossessed. All of the money should have gone directly to the families who were violated.

These are challenging circumstances. Guns in, drugs in, and jobs out. For blacks, the infant mortality rate is higher. Life expectancy is shorter. Unemployment rates often hover at three and four times the national average. There is no policy or plan for reconstruction and for justice. America has vast zones of poverty. Poverty is a weapon of mass destruction.

Why are blacks so good in athletics—baseball, basketball, track, football, and other athletics? For a simple reason: the rules are objective and public and the playing field is even and the goals are clear and the referee is fair and the score is transparent. Under those rules, blacks do amazingly well. In football there are ten yards for all first downs and six points for all touchdowns for all players. But if blacks had to run twelve yards for a touchdown for some social restrictions and whites had to run eight yards for a first down because of some inherited yards, there would be a battle on the ball field. There would be no sense of justice. When blacks have an even playing field, like in athletics, we do very well. But when it comes to access to jobs, education, and health care, the field is very uneven.

When we look at our prison system,[2] blacks are more likely to be stopped, searched, and seized off the street. Stop-and-frisk is an urban policy, where the overwhelming majority of victims were black and brown. But the overwhelming majority of the stopped and frisked were not guilty. Two-and-one-half-million American citizens are in prison. Twenty-five percent of the world's prison population is right here in America. Fifty-five percent of those incarcerated citizens are African American. There are two companies that make $1.2 billion a year off of prisoners' collect telephone calls. There are those in jail for pretrial detention who have been locked up from six months to six years just waiting for trial. We have the growth in prison labor. And so we have the growth of a for-profit prison industrial complex. Not free market capitalism where everyone gets a shot, but immoral cutthroat capitalism where too many of urban Americans are being shot. These are challenging times.

Challenging times require us to put our hands to the plow.

In some churches it is said that lifting your hands up is the highest form of praise. But that is not biblically sound. On the contrary, when Jesus used his hands, he showed us what genuine praise and worship are. If we want to praise the Savior with hands toward heaven but feet on the ground, if we want to worship the Savior in spirit and in truth:

Let's lift somebody up who doesn't have the shoe strings to lift themselves up by their bootstraps.

Let's lift up some stranger who has been beaten down on the Jericho road.

Let's lift up some Lazarus searching for food.

Let's lift up some prostitute facing death by hypocritical unjust judges.

We know Jesus best not by how high he raised his hands but by how far he reached down to lift us up.

Many pick up match sticks and call it heavy lifting; you, Rev. Bracy, pick up the cross, and therefore New Covenant has redeeming power.

New Covenant knows that church is a refueling place with fortification and instruction, not the consummation and the destination. New Covenant knows that religion must wake us up and not be the opiate of the people that puts us to sleep. New Covenant knows that church and religion must not give us a false sense of joy when there is no joy.

And New Covenant knows that the good news of the Savior goes hand-in-hand with politics. Reverend Bracy understands this. He has delved deeply into the politics of Jesus. Yes, Jesus is political in the Bible. Many of us hear the politics of Jesus, and it makes us shiver. We try to separate the birth of Jesus from politics. But no politics, no gospel! Jesus was born and died a Jew connected to Yahweh's intervention, the ancient Jewish deliverance from slavery in Egypt, and the leadership of Moses. Israel comes out of a political emancipation struggle. The only reason they were looking for a messiah who had power was to liberate them from oppression. So Jesus did not limit his emancipation just to his own religion.

If you leave out the Roman occupation (politics), there is nothing left but Santa Claus. You separate the crucifixion (politics), there is nothing left but the Easter Bunny. Jesus understands our situation because we share so much in common. We share in a political system.

Jesus was a Jew in the lineage of the prophets. Jesus was poor. He did not come from the upper class. King Herod was an Israelite in charge of the Jews under occupation. The Pharisees were a high church order, and the Sadducees had status. Jesus was of Palestine and was poor; an ethnic minority. Born under a death warrant, he escaped to Egypt as a refugee. He came up preaching good news to the poor. Jesus healed the brokenhearted and set the political captives free. The day before his crucifixion he stayed in the quarantine shelter of Simon the Leper. Jesus never gave up his relationship with his God, his father, or the poor. That very last night he spent in prison. He had endured two trials and had been accused of treason.

Born ordinary, under conditions subordinary, he rose to become extraordinary.

Jesus's gospel message, his political message, calls us to continue to speak truth to power. Today, there are some adverse politics attempting to turn back the clock, attempting to undermine a half-century of progress. The 2008 moment of redemption faces the 2012 movement of rejection. In 2008 Obama won—redemption. People expressed boundless joy in 2008, and people spoke glowingly beyond racism. In reality, the election of the first black president was beyond Selma, Alabama. Those who were against us in our 1965 Selma campaign to obtain the right to vote were against us in 2008. But this time they were out-voted.[3] In 2008 the sons and daughters of former slaves, the sons and daughters of segregated Selma, could vote. Blacks, eighteen-year-olds, Latinos, women, and students on college campuses are what beat them in 2008. It was not that we were beyond racism; we were beyond Selma. The year 2008 was the fruit of Selma and the 1965 Voting Rights Act, which came out of the Selma campaign. The civil rights movement and Selma opened up America to all citizens of America. We democratized democracy.

At the moment of our redemption (November 4, 2008), when President Obama was declared the winner, I cried. It was the moment when we had won the big one. And I wished Dr. King, Medgar Evers, Fannie Lou Hamer, and Chaney, Goodman, and Schwerner[4] could have been there just for thirty seconds to see the fruit of their labors. I wished for them. I longed for them. And I thought about those who marched in Selma who couldn't afford to be at the Big Party. They were either too poor, injured, or dead. I felt their sacrifices running through my body. I stood there transfixed as I watched Barack Obama come on the stage to declare he had been elected the next president of the United States of America. I cried when I reflected on the joy of the moment and thought about the journey that we traveled to get there. Now the whole world rejoiced. It was the moment, the movement, and the martyrs I thought about.

Now that redemption is facing rejection. Now in 2012 Obama's attempt at reelection faces mean spirited politics—rejection. There are dark clouds brewing, heavy winds coming. There are those willing to sink the ship of America just to destroy the captain, the president. Those on the deck of the ship are celebrating with their billions, while those in the hull of the ship lose everything. We have gone from armed thugs robbing banks to the banks doing the robbing with their masks off in broad daylight. Banks getting bailouts and bonuses while the poor get poorer.

Fifty-three million Americans suffer food insecurity.

Fifty million Americans live in poverty, most of whom work. Those working poor tend to lack savings and are driven into expensive loan schemes.

Twenty-four million survive on food stamps.

Twenty-six million are looking for a job due to plant closings. The same jobs are being exported overseas without exporting the benefits that we in this country fought tooth and nail for, like health care, a minimum wage, etc.

With unemployment rising, we get drugs, guns, and unnecessary wars.

Banks are foreclosing on homes and churches by selling toxic predatory products to minorities, the poor, and uneducated.

Professional politicians commercialize Christianity, but not one super PAC aims at addressing poverty.

Prison labor forces grow to undermine American and immigrant workers.

Student loan debt increases greater than credit card debt.

The Voting Rights Act of 1965 is attacked.

Reverend Bracy knows that Jesus and politics go together because the good news is a living word. It is a living word that calls us to put our hands to work for the lost, the least, and the left out. Pastor Bracy and New Covenant have applied their faith to substance that matters. That is why the people, God's people, search for Rev. Bracy at New Covenant and cry out:

We need leadership when an innocent person is killed; let's check with Pastor Bracy at New Covenant.

We need a sophisticated read on attacks on civil rights and the poor; let's check with New Covenant.

We are losing our houses and churches; let's check with Pastor Bracy.

Because in your witness, your way, and your will you have wrestled with the living word of God, you have become a frame of reference, you have become a landmark, you are the guiding light, and a captain in the fog to those trying to make it to the shore. Many have faith, but it's not attached to substance. Faith without substance is wishful thinking. Faith without substance is creative imagination. But there is no weight attached to faith without substance. Authentic faith is the substance of things hoped for and the evidence of things unseen. Faith without substance means no cross and no sacrifice, no redemption and no caring. Faith without substance; vision without victory.

We had faith in slavery time, but without the substance of the Thirteenth Amendment, we were not set free. That meant we had to engage in battle. We had faith in the back of the bus, but without the substance of public policy; and so Rosa Parks was arrested.

We had faith in Selma, Alabama, but without the substance of the law; we could not vote.

I have seen many church vans with faith ministries advertised on the outside, but seldom faith with political substance in practice.

It is the substance of things hoped for that dares us to struggle.

It is the substance of things hoped for that makes Moses tell Pharaoh, Let my people go, and then tell my people to let Pharaoh go.

It is the substance of saving people that allows Esther to take the risk and to say if I perish let me perish and I am going to see the king.

It is the substance Dr. King dreamed about that changed our circumstances and took him to the mountain top and on to glory.

Reverend Bracy, in the next dimension of your ministry hold fast to faith and substance.

It will get dark sometimes, but God promised never to leave you alone.

It gets lonesome sometime, but he promised to be a company keeper and ever-present help in a time of trouble.

I have been blessed to be in this struggle of substance and faith since I was first jailed fifty-two years ago. I have been blessed to travel the world over, and I have seen a lot of things:

I walked with Dr. King.

I stood in Gandhi's footsteps in India.

I walked and talked with Nelson Mandela. I was with him the Sunday he was freed from jail. I counseled the then-young state senator Barack Obama, who is now president of the United States.

I walked with Cesar Chavez.

I stood by the caskets of some great giants: Dr. King, Cesar Chavez, and Oliver Tambo and witnessed the celebrations of some great triumphs.

There have been ups and downs, mountains and valleys, laughter and tears. And in all I have seen and all I have experienced, I have never seen the righteous forsaken or his seed beg for bread. Hold on when you leave this place, a new morning is coming.

6

My Father's Church

By the rivers of Babylon, there we sat down and there we wept,
When we remembered Zion.
On the willows there, we hung up our harps.
For there our captors asked us for songs, saying,
"Sing us one of the songs of Zion."
How could we sing the Lord's song in a foreign land?
If I forget you, O Jerusalem, let my right hand whither.
Let my tongue cling to the roof of my mouth if I don't remember
*   you, if I do not set Jerusalem above my highest joy.*

Psalm 137:1–6

We thank God for the journey back here again. I first visited South Africa in 1979 to see Nelson Mandela in Cape Town after he was released from prison, and back again in 1994 for his inauguration as president of the new South Africa. I toured the Front Line States[1] in 1985 and returned several times, most recently for Oliver R. Tambo's[2] birthday commemoration and the one-hundredth anniversary celebrations of the African National Congress. Thank you for the award yesterday.

Pray for Mandela and the battled scarred warriors of the struggle. Thank you Pastor Kelley, and My Father's Church.[3] We celebrate nineteen years of freedom—after a long, dark night.

I remember those apartheid years with Oliver Tambo, Frank Chikane, and Johnny Makatini[4]—who made it possible for the trip to occur. At that time we dealt in passbooks, not passports. The apartheid government was stingy to give blacks passports, thus controlling Africans' global connection to the world. But the apartheid government was treacherous in forcing all blacks to carry domestic identity passbooks, thus controlling black South Africans' local connections to other Africans.

During those days, apartheid South Africa was the land of people in exile or in prison, including Oliver R. Tambo and Nelson R. Mandela. Apartheid South Africa flowed with murder and martyrs like Chris Hani and Steve Biko.[5] Leaders were forced under house arrest like Winnie Mandela.[6] Apartheid was real; it was every day, and it was without human rights: abounding fear of false arrest and of tapped phones, no right to vote and never a juror. It diminished our opinions and declared us nonpersons.

But, of course, perfect love casts out fear. It is an *agapic* love, a divine love. It is God's unconditional love that promises us that through the midnight darkness, joy does come in the morning. Apartheid was an old darkness of them-versus-us mentality; today is a new democracy, where South Africa belongs to all who live there.

Today everybody benefited from the struggles in the night. Everybody was a victim. Based on the color of your skin, you could not participate fully in the resources that God had given all who lived in an oppressed land, but a land pregnant with possibilities. At the same time, everybody did *not* contribute to the movement for human rights, civil rights, and a new democratic South Africa.

The prophetic vanguard led the way to a new nonracial, nonsexist democratic South Africa. Looking back we can see how so much weight burdened the backs of those bold marchers and brave martyrs who, without guns and bombs and planes but with a will to dignity, overcame great odds. It was an honor to go to jail for freedom, not for foolishness. You got your stars from your scars.

I once witnessed a conversation of a group of men discussing

Robben Island and what in a real sense it meant to be imprisoned. Some had been left to languish on that Atlantic Ocean Robben Island for thirty-plus years; others for twenty, others for ten. Those that had been there only eight or nine years were limited in their conversation. They didn't have as many scars.

All across apartheid South Africa, not everyone went into exile outside the country; not everyone went underground inside the country. Not everyone joined a liberation group or led massive movements of civil disobedience. Everybody did not endure detention, torture, or so-called accidental suicide by a shoestring while in police custody. During the times I visited South Africa, a land of white power and black pain, I saw many who suffered the brutalities of apartheid. But many, for whatever reason, didn't "walk the walk" against a system that means literally "apartness" and is pronounced literally "apart-hate." As I looked across the landscape of Soweto and Port Elizabeth, Durban and Cape Town, Pretoria and Zululand, I experienced some who had adjusted to apartheid; many resented it, but just a few resisted it. The resistors were a determined minority against the military complex of South Africa, against those countries that openly and secretly propped up apartheid, against those global corporations who defied the worldwide boycott of South Africa, against the number one superpower, the United States government, that removed Nelson Mandela from its terror watch list only in 2008. It was the anti-apartheid minority of risk takers and event shapers who got us to this place of democracy and development.

This was the good prophetic minority. But there was also another minority—the bad perverse minority. The apart-hate system used violence to put the English-speaking and Afrikaner-white minority at the top of the economic and social ladder.

Scripture speaks of being taken away from captivity. Here black South Africa was under captivity, under military occupation, under psychological occupation. This all happened at home.

The majority was made to feel like a minority. You had a minority with all the power; minority with privilege; minority with all the education. You became the majority with pain.

It was more perception than reality. We always had the power, buried deep within. It reminds me of Joshua, sent by Moses to spy out the land of God's promise. They saw everything that God had promised, but the majority report was there were giants in the land. When we look at them we look at ourselves. We feel like grasshoppers. We were not really grasshoppers. But it felt that way.

When we looked in the mirror, we saw a minority. But out the windowpane, we were a majority where all the land belonged to the people.

It was a long, dark night. It's no longer midnight, but it is not yet high noon of a new day. Today we are free, but not equal. Freedom was just a step toward equality. Today you are free but not equal—therefore don't celebrate too soon.

If you are a soccer team on the field and the other team inherited a shorter distance to the goal and got bonus points for making the same goal and their side of the field had grass and your side had rocks, such an inequality would make winning impossible and celebration premature. Skin color apartheid is over. But apartheid still reigns in land ownership, banking, construction, mining and raw materials, health and education, media and communications, jobs and businesses.

In other words, there are miles to go. Your generation has work to do. There needs to be a fight for an even playing field. In today's athletics, when the playing field is even, goals are clear, referees are fair, we can win.

There is no time to waste. Robben Island is not just a place. It's a predicament. Until there is equality where we can compete on an even playing field at home and globally, your call must be for a continuation of the struggle ahead of you, not just a celebration of the struggle behind you. Against the odds of a horrendous system God granted you a measure of victory. I know full well how premature celebration can slow you down.

Back in the United States, African Americans have been number one in presidential politics, number one in athletics, and number one in entertainment. But blacks have also been number one in the prison population, in victims of home foreclosures, in infant mortality, short life expectancy and lack of access to capital.

On this journey we must not celebrate too soon. But if we can make this much progress in the night, think of how much more we can do now that it's morning time. In the end it is the word of God and the promise of God that lift us to a higher level.

I was here in Cape Town that bright Sunday morning when God unleashed the light of Nelson Mandela on the world. When I watched Mandela the prisoner free his jail guards,[7] he out-suffered them. Out-worked them. Out-sacrificed them. Out-prayed them. He was on God's side of history. He chose grace over tanks. He chose reconciliation over retribution.

He used faith as a weapon. He used the power of God within. The kingdom of heaven is at hand. This is the acceptable year of the Lord. Lies couldn't deter it that morning. Jail cells couldn't lock up that morning. Bullets couldn't kill that morning. We hold out until the morning comes. The writer says, "Weeping may endure for a night. But joy cometh in the morning" (Psalm 30:5).

Not just joy. Healing as well.

Amen.

Speeches

Reverend Jesse Jackson has spoken in many places and on important occasions around the world. He has traveled to Africa, South America, Asia, and Europe to give political, religious, and cultural speeches. The venues have ranged from the United Nations in New York to prestigious universities.

Within the United States he has given speeches during key political events, including eight speeches at the Democratic National Convention (DNC) during presidential election years. His speeches illustrate how deeply his vision is embedded in his early engagement in the civil rights movement. His early leadership skills grew in power as he has become a tremendous force within the movement, fighting against racism, sexism, classism, homophobia, and more.

The texts included here provide a small sampling of Rev. Jackson's speeches. They are situated in a powerful political arena that has impacted both the African American community and other marginalized and disenfranchised communities around the world. His speeches indicate the deep desire to fight for equality and justice, not just for African Americans but also for people in all parts of the world. He has had a broader global impact than any other civil rights leader. There probably will never be such an impact again. It is this deep legacy of justice, freedom fighting, and hope that Rev. Jackson leaves for the next generation. He urges all of us to continue the struggle.

7

The Rainbow Nation

**Address to the 1984 Democratic
Party National Convention
San Francisco
July 18, 1984**

Reverend Jackson has spoken at eight Democratic National Conventions. This speech, delivered at the 1984 party convention in San Francisco, followed his first presidential campaign. The nomination went to Vice President Walter Mondale, who lost in the general election to Ronald Reagan.[1]

Tonight we come together bound by our faith in a mighty God, with genuine respect and love for our country, and inheriting the legacy of a great party, the Democratic Party, which is the best hope for redirecting our nation on a more humane, just, and peaceful course.

This is not a perfect party. We are not a perfect people. Yet, we are called to a perfect mission. Our mission: to feed the hungry; to clothe the naked; to house the homeless; to teach the illiterate; to provide jobs for the jobless; and to choose the human race over the nuclear race.

We are gathered here this week to nominate a candidate and adopt a platform which will expand, unify, direct, and inspire our party and the nation to fulfill this mission. My constituency is the desperate, the damned, the disinherited, the disrespected, and the despised. They are restless and seek relief. They have voted in record numbers. They have invested the faith, hope, and trust that they have in us. The Democratic Party must send them a signal that we care. I pledge my best not to let them down.

There is the call of conscience, redemption, expansion, healing, and unity. Leadership must heed the call of conscience, redemption, expansion, healing, and unity, for they are the key to achieving our mission. Time is neutral and does not change things. With courage and initiative, leaders change things.

No generation can choose the age or circumstance in which it is born, but through leadership it can choose to make the age in which it is born an age of enlightenment, an age of jobs, and peace, and justice. Only leadership—that intangible combination of gifts, the discipline, information, circumstance, courage, timing, will, and divine inspiration—can lead us out of the crisis in which we find ourselves. Leadership can mitigate the misery of our nation. Leadership can part the waters and lead our nation in the direction of the Promised Land. Leadership can lift the boats stuck at the bottom.

I have had the rare opportunity to watch seven men, and then two, pour out their souls, offer their service, and heal and heed the call of duty to direct the course of our nation. There is a proper season for everything. There is a time to sow and a time to reap. There's a time to compete and a time to cooperate.

I ask for your vote on the first ballot as a vote for a new direction for this party and this nation—a vote of conviction, a vote of conscience. But I will be proud to support the nominee of this convention for the presidency of the United States of America. Thank you.

Throughout this campaign, I've tried to offer leadership to the Democratic Party and the nation. If, in my high moments, I have done some good, offered some service, shed some light, healed some wounds, rekindled some hope, or stirred someone from apathy and indifference, or in any way along the way helped somebody, then this campaign has not been in vain.

For friends who loved and cared for me, and for a God who

spared me, and for a family who understood, I am eternally grateful.

If, in my low moments, in word, deed, or attitude, through some error of temper, taste, or tone, I have caused anyone discomfort, created pain, or revived someone's fears, that was not my truest self. If there were occasions when my grape turned into a raisin and my joy bell lost its resonance, please forgive me. Charge it to my head and not to my heart. My head—so limited in its finitude; my heart, which is boundless in its love for the human family. I am not a perfect servant. I am a public servant doing my best against the odds. As I develop and serve, be patient. God is not finished with me yet.

This campaign has taught me much: that leaders must be tough enough to fight, tender enough to cry, human enough to make mistakes, humble enough to admit them, strong enough to absorb the pain, and resilient enough to bounce back and keep on moving.

For leaders, the pain is often intense. But you must smile through your tears and keep moving with the faith that there is a brighter side somewhere.

I went to see [former Vice President] Hubert Humphrey three days before he died. He had just called Richard Nixon from his dying bed, and many people wondered why. And I asked him. He said, "Jesse, from this vantage point, the sun is setting in my life, all of the speeches, the political conventions, the crowds, and the great fights are behind me now. At a time like this you are forced to deal with your irreducible essence, forced to grapple with that which is really important to you. And what I've concluded about life," Hubert Humphrey said, "when all is said and done, we must forgive each other, and redeem each other, and move on."

Our party is emerging from one of the hardest fought battles for the Democratic Party's presidential nomination in our history. But our healthy competition should make us better, not bitter. We must use the insight, wisdom, and experience of the late Hubert Humphrey as a balm for the wounds in our party, this nation, and the world. We must forgive each other, redeem each other, regroup, and move on. Our flag is red, white, and blue, but our nation is a rainbow—red, yellow, brown, black, and white—and we're all precious in God's sight.

America is not like a blanket—one piece of unbroken cloth, the same color, the same texture, the same size. America is more like a quilt: many patches, many pieces, many colors, many sizes, all woven and held together by a common thread. The white, the Hispanic, the black, the Arab, the Jew, the woman, the Native American, the small farmer, the businessperson, the environmentalist, the peace activist, the young, the old, the lesbian, the gay, and the disabled make up the American quilt.

Even in our fractured state, all of us count and fit somewhere. We have proven that we can survive without each other. But we have not proven that we can win and make progress without each other. We must come together.

From Fannie Lou Hamer in Atlantic City in 1964 to the Rainbow Coalition in San Francisco today; from the Atlantic to the Pacific, we have experienced pain but progress as we ended American apartheid laws. We got public accommodations. We secured voting rights. We obtained open housing, as young people got the right to vote. We lost Malcolm X, Dr. Martin Luther King Jr., Robert F. Kennedy, John F. Kennedy, and Viola Liuzzo. The team that got us here must be expanded, not abandoned.

Twenty years ago, tears welled up in our eyes as the bodies of [Michael] Schwerner, [Andrew] Goodman, and [James] Chaney were dredged from the depths of a river in Mississippi. Twenty years later, our communities, black and Jewish, are in anguish, anger, and pain. Feelings have been hurt on both sides. There is a crisis in communication. Confusion is in the air. But we cannot afford to lose our way. We may agree to agree, or agree to disagree on issues; we must bring back civility to these tensions.

We are copartners in a long and rich religious history—the Judeo-Christian tradition. Many blacks and Jews have a shared passion for social justice at home and peace abroad. We must seek a revival of the spirit, inspired by a new vision and new possibilities. We must return to higher ground. We are bound by Moses and Jesus, but also connected with Islam and Muhammad. These three great religions, Judaism, Christianity, and Islam, were all born in the revered and holy city of Jerusalem.

We are bound by Dr. Martin Luther King Jr. and Rabbi Abraham Heschel, crying out from their graves for us to reach common ground. We are bound by shared blood and shared sacrifices. We are much too intelligent, much too bound by our Judeo-Christian heritage, much too victimized by racism, sexism, militarism, and anti-Semitism, much too threatened as historical scapegoats to go on divided one from another. We must turn from finger pointing to clasped hands. We must share our burdens and our joys with each other once again. We must turn to each other and not on each other and choose higher ground.

Twenty years later, we cannot be satisfied by just restoring the old coalition. Old wine skins must make room for new wine. We must heal and expand. The Rainbow Coalition is making room for Arab Americans. They, too, know the pain and hurt of racial and religious rejection. They must not continue to be made pariahs. The Rainbow Coalition is making room for Hispanic Americans, who this very night are living under the threat of the Simpson-Mazzoli Act,[2] and for farm workers from Ohio who are fighting the Campbell Soup Company with a boycott to achieve legitimate workers' rights.

The Rainbow is making room for the Native American, the most exploited people of all, a people with the greatest moral claim among us. We support them as they seek the restoration of their ancient land and claim among us. We support them as they seek the restoration of land and water rights, as they seek to preserve their ancestral homeland and the beauty of a land that was once all theirs. They can never receive a fair share for all they have given us. They must finally have a fair chance to develop their great resources and to preserve their people and their culture.

The Rainbow Coalition includes Asian Americans, now being killed in our streets—scapegoats for the failures of corporate, industrial, and economic policies.

The Rainbow is making room for young Americans. Twenty years ago, our young people were dying in a war for which they could not even vote. Twenty years later, young America has the power to stop a war in Central America and the responsibility to vote in great numbers. Young America must be politically active in 1984. The choice is war or peace. We must make room for young America.

The Rainbow includes disabled veterans. The color scheme fits in the Rainbow. The disabled have their handicap revealed and their genius concealed, while the able-bodied have their genius revealed and their disability concealed. But ultimately, we must judge people by their values and their contribution. Don't leave anybody out. I would rather have Roosevelt in a wheelchair than Reagan on a horse.

The Rainbow is making room for small farmers. They have suffered tremendously under the Reagan regime. They will either receive 90 percent parity or 100 percent charity. We must address their concerns and make room for them. The Rainbow includes lesbians and gays. No American citizen ought to be denied equal protection under the law.

We must be unusually committed and caring as we expand our family to include new members. All of us must be tolerant and understanding as the fears and anxieties of the rejected and the party leadership express themselves in many different ways. Too often what we call hate—as if it were some deeply rooted philosophy or strategy—is simply ignorance, anxiety, paranoia, fear, and insecurity. To be strong leaders, we must be long-suffering as we seek to right the wrongs of our party and our nation. We must expand our party, heal our party, and unify our party. That is our mission in 1984.

We are often reminded that we live in a great nation—and we do. But it can be greater still. The Rainbow is mandating a new definition of greatness. We must not measure greatness from the mansion down, but the manger up. Jesus said that we should not be judged by the bark we wear but by the fruit that we bear. Jesus said that we must measure greatness by how we treat the least of these.

Rising tides don't lift all boats, particularly those stuck at the bottom. For the boats stuck at the bottom there's a misery index. This administration has made life more miserable for the poor. Its attitude has been contemptuous. Its policies and programs have been cruel and unfair to working people. They must be held accountable in November for increasing infant mortality among the poor.

Mr. Reagan will ask us to pray, and I believe in prayer. I have come to this way by the power of prayer. But then, we must watch false prophecy. He cuts energy assistance to the poor, cuts breakfast programs from children, cuts lunch programs from children, cuts job training from children, and then says to an empty table, "Let us pray." Apparently, he is not familiar with the structure of a prayer. You thank the Lord for the food that you are about to receive, not the food that just left. I think that we should pray, but don't pray for the food that left. Pray for the man that took the food to leave. We need a change. We need a change in November.

Democracy guarantees opportunity, not success.

Democracy guarantees the right to participate, not a license for either a majority or a minority to dominate.

The victory for the Rainbow Coalition in the platform debates today was not whether we won or lost but that we raised the right issues. We could afford to lose the vote; issues are nonnegotiable. We could not afford to avoid raising the right questions. Our self-respect and our moral integrity were at stake. Our heads are perhaps bloody, but not bowed. Our back is straight. We can go home and face our people. Our vision is clear.

When we think, on this journey from slave ship to championship, that we have gone from the planks of the Boardwalk in Atlantic City in 1964 to fighting to help write the planks in the platform in San Francisco in '84, there is a deep and abiding sense of joy in our souls in spite of the tears in our eyes. Though there are missing planks, there is a solid foundation on which to build. Our party can win, but we must provide hope which will inspire people to struggle and achieve; provide a plan that shows a way out of our dilemma and then lead the way.

For all of our joy and excitement, we must not save the world and lose our souls. We should never short-circuit enforcing the Voting Rights Act at every level. When one of us rises, all of us will rise. Justice is the way out. Peace is the way out. We should not act as if nuclear weaponry is negotiable and debatable.

There is a way out—jobs. Put America back to work. When I was a child growing up in Greenville, South Carolina, the Reverend Sample used to preach every so often a sermon relating to Jesus. And he said, "If I be lifted up, I'll draw all men unto me." As a child growing up, I didn't quite understand what he meant, but I understand a little better now. If you raise up truth, it's magnetic. It has a way of drawing people.

With all this confusion in this convention, the bright lights and parties and big fun, we must raise up the simple proposition: If we lift up a program to feed the hungry, they'll come running; if we lift up a program to study war no more, our youth will come running; if we lift up a program to put America back to work, and an alternative to welfare and despair, they will come working.

If we cut that military budget without cutting our defense, and use that money to rebuild bridges and put steel workers back to work, and use that money and provide jobs for our cities, and use that money to build schools and pay teachers and educate our children and build hospitals and train doctors and train nurses, the whole nation will come running to us.

As I leave you now, we vote in this convention and get ready to go back across this nation in a couple of days. In this campaign, I've tried to be faithful to my promise. I lived in old barrios, ghettos, and reservations and housing projects. I have a message for our youth. I challenge them to put hope in their brains and not dope in their veins. I told them that like Jesus, I, too, was born in the slum. But just because you're born in the slum does not mean the slum is born in you, and you can rise above it if your mind is made up.

I told them in every slum there are two sides. When I see a broken window—that's the slummy side. Train some youth to become a glazier—that's the sunny side. When I see a missing brick—that's the slummy side. Let that child in the union and become a brick mason and build—that's the sunny side. When I see a missing door—that's the slummy side. Train some youth to become a carpenter—that's the sunny side. And when I see the vulgar words and hieroglyphics of destitution on the walls—that's the slummy side. Train some youth to become a painter, an artist—that's the sunny side.

We leave this place looking for the sunny side because there's a brighter side somewhere. I'm more convinced than ever that we can win. We will vault up the rough side of the mountain. We can win. I just want young America to do me one favor, just one favor. Exercise the right to dream. You must face reality—that which is. But then dream of a reality that ought to be—that must be. Live beyond the pain of reality with the dream of a bright tomorrow. Use hope and imagination as weapons of survival and progress. Use love to motivate you and obligate you to serve the human family.

Young America, dream. Choose the human race over the nuclear race. Bury the weapons and don't burn the people. Dream—dream of a new value system. Teachers who teach for life and not just for a living; teach because they can't help it. Dream of lawyers more concerned about justice than a judgeship. Dream of doctors more concerned about public health than personal wealth. Dream of preachers and priests who will prophesy and not just profiteer. Preach and dream!

Our time has come. Our time has come. Suffering breeds character. Character breeds faith. In the end, faith will not disappoint.

Our time has come. Our faith, hope, and dreams will prevail. Our time has come. Weeping has endured for nights, but now joy cometh in the morning.

Our time has come. No grave can hold our body down. Our time has come. No lie can live forever.

Our time has come. We must leave racial battleground and

8

Common Ground

This speech at the 1988 convention in Atlanta followed Rev. Jackson's second campaign for the presidential nomination. At the convention, Michael Dukakis, governor of Massachusetts, received the party nomination but went on to lose the general election to Vice President George H. W. Bush.

Tonight, we pause and give praise and honor to God for being good enough to allow us to be at this place at this time. When I look out at this convention, I see the face of America: red, yellow, brown, black, and white. We're all precious in God's sight—the real rainbow coalition.

All of us—all of us who are here think that we are seated. But we're really standing on someone's shoulders. Ladies and gentlemen, Mrs. Rosa Parks—the mother of the civil rights movement. [*Mrs. Rosa Parks is brought to the podium.*]

I want to express my deep love and appreciation for the support my family has given me over these past months. They have endured pain, anxiety, threat, and fear. But they have been strengthened and made secure by our faith in God, in America, and in you. Your love has protected us and made us strong. To my wife, Jackie, the foundation of our family; to our five children, whom you met tonight;

to my mother, Mrs. Helen Jackson, who is present tonight; and to our grandmother, Mrs. Matilda Burns; to my brother Chuck and his family; to my mother-in-law, Mrs. Gertrude Brown, who just last month at age sixty-one graduated from Hampton Institute—a marvelous achievement.

I offer my appreciation to Mayor Andrew Young, who has provided such gracious hospitality to all of us this week.

And a special salute to President Jimmy Carter. President Carter restored honor to the White House after Watergate. He gave many of us a special opportunity to grow. For his kind words, for his unwavering commitment to peace in the world, I offer my special thanks.

My right and my privilege to stand here before you has been won—in my lifetime—by the blood and the sweat of the innocent.

Twenty-four years ago, the late Fannie Lou Hamer and Aaron Henry—who sits here tonight from Mississippi—were locked out on the streets in Atlantic City, the head of the Mississippi Freedom Democratic Party.[1] But tonight, a black and white delegation from Mississippi is headed by Ed Cole, a black man from Mississippi, twenty-four years later.

Many were lost in the struggle for the right to vote: Jimmy Lee Jackson, a young student, gave his life; Viola Liuzzo, a white mother from Detroit, called "nigger lover," had her brains blown out at point-blank range; [Michael] Schwerner, [Andrew] Goodman and [James] Chaney—two white Jews and a black—found in a common grave, bodies riddled with bullets in Mississippi; the four darling little girls in a church in Birmingham, Alabama. They died that we might have a right to live.

Dr. Martin Luther King Jr. lies only a few miles from us tonight. Tonight he must feel good as he looks down upon us. We sit here together, a rainbow, a coalition—the sons and daughters of slave masters and the sons and daughters of slaves, sitting together around a common table, to decide the direction of our party and our country. His heart would be full tonight.

As a testament to the struggles of those who have gone before;

as a legacy for those who will come after; as a tribute to the endurance, the patience, the courage of our forefathers and mothers; as an assurance that their prayers are being answered, that their work has not been in vain, and that hope is eternal, tomorrow night my name will go into nomination for the presidency of the United States of America.

We meet tonight at the crossroad, a point of decision. Shall we expand, be inclusive, find unity and power; or suffer division and impotence?

We've come to Atlanta, the cradle of the Old South, the crucible of the New South. Tonight, there is a sense of celebration, because we are moved, fundamentally moved from racial battlegrounds by law, to economic common ground. Tomorrow we'll be challenged to move to higher ground.

Common ground. Think of Jerusalem, the intersection where many trails met. A small village that became the birthplace for three great religions—Judaism, Christianity, and Islam. Why was this village so blessed? Because it provided a crossroad where different people met, different cultures, different civilizations could meet and find common ground. When people come together, flowers always flourish—the air is rich with the aroma of a new spring.

Take New York, the dynamic metropolis. What makes New York so special? It's the invitation at the Statue of Liberty, "Give me your tired, your poor, your huddled masses who yearn to breathe free." Not restricted to English only. Many people, many cultures, many languages with one thing in common: They yearn to breathe free. Common ground.

Tonight in Atlanta, for the first time in this century, we convene in the South; a state where governors once stood in school-house doors; where Julian Bond was denied a seat in the state legislature because of his conscientious objection to the Vietnam War; a city that, through its five black universities, has graduated more black students than any city in the world. Atlanta, now a modern intersection of the New South.

Common ground. That's the challenge of our party tonight—left wing, right wing.

Progress will not come through boundless liberalism nor static conservatism, but at the critical mass of mutual survival. It takes two wings to fly. Whether you're a hawk or a dove, you're just a bird living in the same environment, in the same world.

The Bible teaches that when lions and lambs lie down together, none will be afraid, and there will be peace in the valley. It sounds impossible. Lions eat lambs. Lambs sensibly flee from lions. Yet even lions and lambs find common ground. Why? Because neither lions nor lambs want the forest to catch on fire. Neither lions nor lambs want acid rain to fall. Neither lions nor lambs can survive nuclear war. If lions and lambs can find common ground, surely we can as well—as civilized people.

The only time that we win is when we come together. In 1960, John Kennedy, the late John Kennedy, beat Richard Nixon by only 112,000 votes—less than one vote per precinct. He won by the margin of our hope. He brought us together. He reached out. He had the courage to defy his advisors and inquire about Dr. King's jailing in Albany, Georgia. We won by the margin of our hope, inspired by courageous leadership. In 1964, Lyndon Johnson brought both wings together—the thesis, the antithesis, and the creative synthesis—and together we won. In 1976, Jimmy Carter unified us again, and we won. When we do not come together, we never win. In 1968, the division and despair in July led to our defeat in November. In 1980, rancor in the spring and the summer led to Reagan in the fall. When we divide, we cannot win. We must find common ground as the basis for survival and development and change and growth.

Today when we debated, differed, deliberated, agreed to agree, agreed to disagree, when we had the good judgment to argue a case and then not self-destruct, George Bush was just a little further away from the White House and a little closer to private life.

Tonight, I salute Governor Michael Dukakis. He has run—he has run a well-managed and a dignified campaign. No matter how tired or how tried, he always resisted the temptation to stoop to demagoguery.

I've watched a good mind fast at work, with steel nerves, guiding his campaign out of the crowded field without appeal to the worst in us. I've watched his perspective grow as his environment has expanded. I've seen his toughness and tenacity close up. I know his commitment to public service. Mike Dukakis's parents were a doctor and a teacher; my parents a maid, a beautician, and a janitor. There's a great gap between Brookline, Massachusetts, and Haney Street in the Fieldcrest Village housing projects in Greenville, South Carolina.

He studied law; I studied theology. There are differences of religion, region, and race; differences in experiences and perspectives. But the genius of America is that out of the many we become one.

Providence has enabled our paths to intersect. His foreparents came to America on immigrant ships; my foreparents came to America on slave ships. But whatever the original ships, we're in the same boat tonight.

Our ships could pass in the night—if we have a false sense of independence—or they could collide and crash. We would lose our passengers. We can seek a high reality and a greater good. Apart, we can drift on the broken pieces of Reaganomics, satisfy our baser instincts, and exploit the fears of our people. At our highest, we can call upon noble instincts and navigate this vessel to safety. The greater good is the common good.

As Jesus said, "Not my will, but thine be done." It was his way of saying there's a higher good beyond personal comfort or position.

The good of our nation is at stake. It's commitment to working men and women, to the poor and the vulnerable, to the many in the world.

With so many guided missiles, and so much misguided leadership, the stakes are exceedingly high. Our choice? Full participation in a democratic government or more abandonment and neglect. And so this night, we choose not a false sense of independence, not our capacity to survive and endure. Tonight we choose interdependency, and our capacity to act and unite for the greater good.

Common good is finding commitment to new priorities of expansion and inclusion. A commitment to expanded participation in the Democratic Party at every level. A commitment to a shared national campaign strategy and involvement at every level.

A commitment to new priorities that ensure that hope will be kept alive. A common-ground commitment to a legislative agenda for empowerment, for the John Conyers bill—universal, on-site, same-day registration everywhere. A commitment to DC statehood and empowerment—DC deserves statehood. A commitment to economic set-asides, commitment to the [Ron] Dellums bill for comprehensive sanctions against South Africa. A shared commitment to a common direction.

Common ground.

Easier said than done. Where do you find common ground? At the point of challenge. This campaign has shown that politics need not be marketed by politicians, packaged by pollsters and pundits. Politics can be a moral arena where people come together to find common ground.

We find common ground at the plant gate that closes on workers without notice. We find common ground at the farm auction, where a good farmer loses his or her land to bad loans or diminishing markets. Common ground at the school yard where teachers cannot get adequate pay, and students cannot get a scholarship, and can't make a loan. Common ground at the hospital admitting room, where somebody tonight is dying because they cannot afford to go upstairs to a bed that's empty, waiting for someone with insurance to get sick. We are a better nation than that. We must do better.

Common ground. What is leadership if not present help in a time of crisis? And so I met you at the point of challenge. In Jay, Maine, where paper workers were striking for fair wages; in Greenville, Iowa, where family farmers struggle for a fair price; in Cleveland, Ohio, where working women seek comparable worth; in

McFarland, California, where the children of Hispanic farm work-ers may be dying from poisoned land, dying in clusters with can-cer; in an AIDS hospice in Houston, Texas, where the sick support one another, too often rejected by their own parents and friends.

Common ground. America is not a blanket woven from one thread, one color, one cloth. When I was a child growing up in Greenville, South Carolina, and Grandmamma could not afford a blanket, she didn't complain and we did not freeze. Instead she took pieces of old cloth—patches, wool, silk, gabardine, croker sack—only patches, barely good enough to wipe off your shoes with. But they didn't stay that way very long. With sturdy hands and a strong cord, she sewed them together into a quilt, a thing of beauty and power and culture. Now, Democrats, we must build such a quilt.

Farmers, you seek fair prices and you are right—but you cannot stand alone. Your patch is not big enough.

Workers, you fight for fair wages, you are right—but your patch labor is not big enough.

Women, you seek comparable worth and pay equity, you are right—but your patch is not big enough.

Women, mothers, who seek Head Start, and day care, and pre-natal care on the front side of life, relevant jail care and welfare on the back side of life, you are right—but your patch is not big enough.

Students, you seek scholarships, you are right—but your patch is not big enough.

Blacks and Hispanics, when we fight for civil rights, we are right—but our patch is not big enough.

Gays and lesbians, when you fight against discrimination and a cure for AIDS, you are right—but your patch is not big enough.

Conservatives and progressives, when you fight for what you believe, right wing, left wing, hawk, dove, you are right from your point of view, but your point of view is not enough.

But don't despair. Be as wise as my Grandmamma. Pull the patches and the pieces together, bound by a common thread.

When we form a great quilt of unity and common ground, we'll have the power to bring about health care and housing and jobs and education and hope to our nation.

We, the people, can win.

We stand at the end of a long, dark night of reaction. We stand tonight united in the commitment to a new direction. For almost eight years we've been led by those who view social good coming from private interest, who view public life as a means to increase private wealth. They have been prepared to sacrifice the common good of the many to satisfy the private interests and the wealth of a few.

We believe in a government that's a tool of our democracy in service to the public, not an instrument of the aristocracy in search of private wealth. We believe in government with the consent of the governed, "of, for and by the people." We must now emerge into a new day with a new direction.

Reaganomics: Based on the belief that the rich had too little money and the poor had too much. That's classic Reaganomics. They believe that the poor had too much money and the rich had too little money, so they engaged in reverse Robin Hood: took from the poor, gave to the rich, paid for by the middle class. We cannot stand four more years of Reaganomics in any version, in any disguise.

How do I document that case? Seven years later, the richest 1 percent of our society pays 20 percent less in taxes. The poorest 10 percent pay 20 percent more: Reaganomics.

Reagan gave the rich and the powerful a multibillion-dollar party. Now the party is over. He expects the people to pay for the damage. I take this principal position, convention, let us not raise taxes on the poor and the middle class; but those who had the party, the rich and the powerful, must pay for the party.

I just want to take common sense to high places. We're spending $150 billion a year defending Europe and Japan forty-three years after the war is over. We have more troops in Europe tonight than we had seven years ago. Yet the threat of war is ever more remote.

Germany and Japan are now creditor nations; that means they've got a surplus. We are a debtor nation—means we are in debt. Let them share more of the burden of their own defense. Use some of that money to build decent housing. Use some of that money to educate our children. Use some of that money for long-term health care. Use some of that money to wipe out these slums and put America back to work!

I just want to take common sense to high places. If we can bail out Europe and Japan; if we can bail out Continental Bank and Chrysler—and Mr. Lee Iacocca [chairman of Chrysler] makes $8,000 an hour—we can bail out the family farmer.

I just want to make common sense. It does not make sense to close down 650 thousand family farms in this country while importing food from abroad subsidized by the US government. Let's make sense.

It does not make sense to be escorting all our tankers up and down the Persian Gulf paying $2.50 for every $1 worth of oil we bring out, while oil wells are capped in Texas, Oklahoma, and Louisiana. I just want to make sense.

Leadership must meet the moral challenge of its day. What's the moral challenge of our day? We have public accommodations. We have the right to vote. We have open housing. What's the fundamental challenge of our day? It is to end economic violence. Plant closings without notice—economic violence. Even the greedy do not profit long from greed—economic violence.

Most poor people are not lazy. They are not black. They are not brown. They are mostly white and female and young. But whether white, black, or brown, a hungry baby's belly turned inside out is the same color—color it pain; color it hurt; color it agony.

Most poor people are not on welfare. Some of them are illiterate and can't read the want-ad sections. And when they can, they can't find a job that matches the address. They work hard every day.

I know. I live among them. I'm one of them. I know they work. I'm a witness. They catch the early bus. They work every day.

They raise other people's children. They work every day.

They clean the streets. They work every day. They drive dangerous cabs. They work every day. They change the beds you slept in in these hotels last night and can't get a union contract. They work every day.

No, no, they are not lazy! Someone must defend them because it's right, and they cannot speak for themselves. They work in hospitals. I know they do. They wipe the bodies of those who are sick with fever and pain. They empty their bedpans. They clean out their commodes. No job is beneath them, and yet when they get sick they cannot lie in the bed they made up every day. America, that is not right. We are a better nation than that. We are a better nation than that.

We need a real war on drugs. You can't "just say no." It's deeper than that. You can't just get a palm reader or an astrologer. It's more profound than that.

We are spending $150 billion on drugs a year. We've gone from ignoring this fact to focusing on the children. Children cannot buy $150 billion worth of drugs a year; a few high-profile athletes are not laundering $150 billion a year—bankers are.

I met the children in Watts. Unfortunately, in their despair, their grapes of hope have become raisins of despair, and they're turning on each other and they're self-destructing. But I stayed with them all night long. I wanted to hear their case.

They said, "Jesse Jackson, as you challenge us to say no to drugs, you're right; and to not sell them, you're right; and not use these guns, you're right. But we have neither jobs nor houses nor services nor training—no way out. Some of us take drugs as anesthesia for our pain. Some take drugs as a way of pleasure, good short-term pleasure and long-term pain. Some sell drugs to make money. It's wrong, we know, but you need to know that we know. We can go and buy the drugs by the boxes at the port. If we can buy the drugs at the port, don't you believe the federal government can stop it if they want to?"

They say, "We don't have Saturday night specials anymore." They say, "We buy AK-47s and Uzis, the latest make of weapons. We buy them along these boulevards."

You cannot fight a war on drugs unless and until you're going to challenge the bankers and the gun sellers and those who grow them. Don't just focus on the children; let's stop drugs at the level of supply and demand. We must end the scourge on the American culture.

Leadership. What difference will we make? Leadership. Cannot just go along to get along. We must do more than change presidents. We must change direction.

Leadership must face the moral challenge of our day. The nuclear war build-up is irrational. Strong leadership cannot desire to look tough and let that stand in the way of the pursuit of peace. Leadership must reverse the arms race. At least we should pledge no first use. Why? Because first use begets first retaliation. And that's mutual annihilation. That's not a rational way out.

No use at all. Let's think it out and not fight it out because it's an unwinnable fight. Why hold a card that you can never drop? Let's give peace a chance.

Leadership. We now have this marvelous opportunity to have a breakthrough with the Soviets. Last year two hundred thousand Americans visited the Soviet Union. There's a chance for joint ventures into space—not star wars and war arms escalation but a space defense initiative. Let's build in space together and demilitarize the heavens. There's a way out.

America, let us expand. When Mr. Reagan and Mr. Gorbachev met there was a big meeting. They represented together one-eighth of the human race. Seven-eighths of the human race was locked out of that room. Most people in the world tonight—half are Asian, one-half of them are Chinese. There are twenty-two nations in the Middle East. There's Europe; forty million Latin Americans next door to us; the Caribbean; Africa—a half-billion people.

Most people in the world today are yellow or brown or black, non-Christian, poor, female, young, and don't speak English in the real world.

This generation must offer leadership to the real world. We're losing ground in Latin America, the Middle East, South Africa, because we're not focusing on the real world. That's the real world.

We must use basic principles—support international law. We stand the most to gain from it. Support human rights—we believe in that. Support self-determination—we're built on that. Support economic development—you know it's right. Be consistent and gain our moral authority in the world. I challenge you tonight, my friends, let's be bigger and better as a nation and as a party.

We have basic challenges—freedom in South Africa. We've already agreed as Democrats to declare South Africa to be a terrorist state. But don't just stop there. Get South Africa out of Angola; free Namibia; support the front-line states. We must have a new humane, consistent human rights policy in Africa.

I'm often asked, "Jesse, why do you take on these tough issues? They're not very political. We can't win that way."

If an issue is morally right, it will eventually be political. It may be political and never be right. Fannie Lou Hamer didn't have the most votes in Atlantic City, but her principles have outlasted every delegate who voted to lock her out. Rosa Parks did not have the most votes, but she was morally right. Dr. King didn't have the most votes about the Vietnam War, but he was morally right. If we are principled first, our politics will fall in place.

"Jesse, why do you take these big bold initiatives?" A poem by an unknown author went something like this: "We mastered the air, we conquered the sea, annihilated distance and prolonged life, but we're not wise enough to live on this earth without war and without hate."

As for Jesse Jackson, Daisy Rinehart writes:

I'm tired of sailing my little boat,
Far inside the harbor bar.
I want to go out where the big ships float,
Out on the deep
where the great ones are.
And should my frail craft
prove too slight
For waves that sweep those billows o'er,

I'd rather go down in the stirring fight
Than drown to death
at the sheltered shore."

We've got to go out, my friends, where the big boats are.

And then for our children. Young America, hold your head high now. We can win. We must not lose you to drugs and violence, premature pregnancy, suicide, cynicism, pessimism, and despair. We can win. Wherever you are tonight, I challenge you to hope and to dream. Don't submerge your dreams. Exercise above all else, even on drugs, dream of the day you are drug free. Even in the gutter, dream of the day that you will be up on your feet again.

You must never stop dreaming. Face reality, yes, but don't stop with the way things are. Dream of things as they ought to be. Dream. Face pain, but love, hope, faith, and dreams will help you rise above the pain. Use hope and imagination as weapons of survival and progress, but you keep on dreaming, young America. Dream of peace. Peace is rational and reasonable. War is irrational in this age, and unwinnable.

Dream of teachers who teach for life and not for a living. Dream of doctors who are concerned more about public health than private wealth. Dream of lawyers more concerned about justice than a judgeship. Dream of preachers who are concerned more about prophecy than profiteering. Dream on the high road with sound values.

And then America, as we go forth to September, October, November, and then beyond, America must never surrender to a high moral challenge.

Do not surrender to drugs. The best drug policy is a "no first use." Don't surrender with needles and cynicism. Let's have "no first use" on the one hand, or clinics on the other. Never surrender, young America. Go forward.

America must never surrender to malnutrition. We can feed the hungry and clothe the naked. We must never surrender. We must go forward.

We must never surrender to illiteracy. Invest in our children. Never surrender; and go forward. We must never surrender to inequality. Women cannot compromise on ERA [the Equal Rights Amendment] or comparable worth. Women are making 60 cents on the dollar to what a man makes. Women cannot buy meat cheaper. Women cannot buy bread cheaper. Women cannot buy milk cheaper. Women deserve to get paid for the work that you do. It's right! And it's fair.

Don't surrender, my friends. Those who have AIDS tonight, you deserve our compassion. Even with AIDS you must not surrender.

In your wheelchairs. I see you sitting here tonight in those wheelchairs. I've stayed with you. I've reached out to you across our nation. And don't you give up. I know it's tough sometimes. People look down on you. It took you a little more effort to get here tonight. And no one should look down on you, but sometimes mean people do. The only justification we have for looking down on someone is that we're going to stop and pick them up.

But even in your wheelchairs, don't you give up. We cannot forget fifty years ago when our backs were against the wall, Roosevelt was in a wheelchair. I would rather have Roosevelt in a wheelchair than Reagan and Bush on a horse. Don't you surrender and don't you give up. Don't surrender and don't give up!

Why can't I challenge you this way? "Jesse Jackson, you don't understand my situation. You be on television. You don't understand. I see you with the big people. You don't understand my situation."

I understand. You see me on TV, but you don't know the *me* that makes me, *me*. They wonder, "Why does Jesse run?" because they see me running for the White House. They don't see the house I'm running from.

I have a story. I wasn't always on television. Writers were not always outside my door. When I was born late one afternoon, October 8, in Greenville, South Carolina, no writers asked my mother her name. Nobody chose to write down our address. My mama was not supposed to make it, and I was not supposed to make it. You see, I was born of a teenage mother, who was born of a teenage mother.

I understand. I know abandonment, and people being mean to you, and saying you're nothing and nobody and can never be anything.

I understand. Jesse Jackson is my third name. I'm adopted. When I had no name, my grandmother gave me her name. My name was Jesse Burns 'til I was twelve. So I wouldn't have a blank space, she gave me a name to hold me over. I understand when nobody knows your name. I understand when you have no name.

I understand. I wasn't born in the hospital. Mama didn't have insurance. I was born in the bed at [the] house. I really do understand. Born in a three-room house, bathroom in the backyard, slop jar by the bed, no hot and cold running water. I understand. Wallpaper used for decoration? No. For a windbreaker. I understand. I'm a working person's person. That's why I understand you whether you're black or white. I understand work. I was not born with a silver spoon in my mouth. I had a shovel programmed for my hand.

My mother, a working woman. So many of the days she went to work early, with runs in her stockings. She knew better, but she wore runs in her stockings so that my brother and I could have matching socks and not be laughed at in school. I understand.

At three o'clock on Thanksgiving Day, we couldn't eat turkey because Mamma was preparing somebody else's turkey at three o'clock. We had to play football to entertain ourselves. And then around six o'clock she would get off the Alta Vista bus, and we would bring up the leftovers and eat our turkey—leftovers, the carcass, the cranberries—around eight o'clock at night. I really do understand.

Every one of these funny labels they put on you, those of you who are watching this broadcast tonight in the projects, on the corners, I understand. Call you outcast, low down, you can't make it, you're nothing, you're from nobody, subclass, underclass; when you see Jesse Jackson, when my name goes in nomination, your name goes in nomination.

I was born in the slum, but the slum was not born in me. And it wasn't born in you, and you can make it.

Wherever you are tonight, you can make it. Hold your head high; stick your chest out. You can make it. It gets dark sometimes, but the morning comes. Don't you surrender!

Suffering breeds character; character breeds faith. In the end faith will not disappoint.

You must not surrender! You may or may not get there, but just know that you're qualified! And you hold on, and hold out! We must never surrender!! America will get better and better.

Keep hope alive. Keep hope alive! Keep hope alive! On tomorrow night and beyond, keep hope alive!

I love you very much. I love you very much.

9

From Slavery to Freedom: Leveling the Playing Field

Annual Conference of the Rainbow PUSH Coalition Chicago, Illinois July 21, 2002

Our theme, "From Slavery to Freedom: Leveling the Playing Field," reflects the true journey of the United States of America to become "a more perfect Union." There is a historical context to what we are witnessing today. We are a nation built upon the transatlantic slave trade and the institution of slavery.[1] That history endured from 1619, with the arrival of the first group of twenty Africans brought by force to Jamestown, Virginia, to the forced end of slavery in 1865, after the Civil War. By 1815, cotton was the most valuable product America exported. By 1860, on the eve of the Civil War, the dollar value of the American property of our foreparents who were enslaved was greater than that of all of America's railroads, all of America's banks, and all of America's factories combined. In the seventy-two years between the presidencies of George Washington and Abraham Lincoln, slaveholders controlled the White House for at least fifty years.

Wall Street was built on the shipping industry and commodities exchange. Our foreparents from Africa were the commodities being shipped. There is an African graveyard on Wall Street, a standing memorial to its roots. Anthropologists have shown the marks on our ancestors' backs, shoulders, and heads reflecting the violence, heavy lifting, and endless toil they were forced to endure.

On the one hand, race was the ideology, but greed was the motivation. And that greed exploited everything in its path: Chinese indentured servants; Eastern European miners; women; people from Mexico; Native Americans' lands; a race divide and a class divide; manipulation and exploitation. Greed and mean-spiritedness have been the real competitors with the noble theory of democracy, open, free and fair elections, transparency, one set of rules, equal protection, and balance of power. These principles are constantly under threat by race and class manipulation. Now the greed of global capital has outdistanced democratic governments as well as labor, environmental, and human rights protections. The American value that a human being is a commodity to be used for capital accumulation goes back to the origin of the nation. Under slavery, Africans and African Americans were seen as livestock and work tools. From this race and class divide a small group of elite families have come to dominate the politics and economics of our country. Slaves worked the land, but the master got the money.

The history of the institution of slavery must be taught as core curriculum in American schools, colleges, and universities. The slavery of black bodies is the very foundation of American identity and wealth. It was once called slavery—today it is called a skin tax. People of color suffer disproportionately all the negative indications that hurt their quality of life. It is not that they don't work hard. It is not that they don't have dreams for their children. It is simply because of the color of their skin.

African Americans, Latinos, Asian and Native Americans pay more for basic living items: mortgage lending, car, bank loans, housing, taxes, and health care. We work more and get paid less. This predatory economic race profiling is a pernicious burden. It adds to stress, limiting life options and reducing life expectancy. We deserve equal protection under the law. But there is a closed-door, no-talk policy, a calculated political indifference to our rights and needs.

In this context we convene today.

Since we last met we have witnessed the shattering of our national confidence with an external attack of September 11, 2001, carried out by Osama bin Laden and his al-Qaeda group. As a nation we have shared outrage and mourning and unified as a people against terrorism. But we are now witnessing an already erratic foreign policy becoming incomprehensible. Foreign policy should not be foreign to democratic principles, international law, human rights, self-determination, peaceful coexistence, economic justice, and fair rules.

The threatened misadventure into Iraq is being discouraged by the European Union, African Union, and Arab states. The president and vice president of the United States are inching toward invading Iraq. But there is no connection between the government of Iraq and the September 11 tragedy. Osama bin Laden evades US capture, but Iraq has the oil. Weapons of mass destruction—no. Oil refineries—yes.[2] Our unilateral, isolationist, and preemptive policies are not making us more secure; instead, they are increasing our vulnerability and making the region and the world less secure. Our allies have challenged our approach. The very forces that we choose not to engage, not to talk with—Iran, Iraq, Libya, Cuba, and North Korea—are still forces to be reckoned with and not ignored. We still must have a "one-big-tent" view of the world. Talking with your adversary is not a sign of agreement or weakness; it's just the most effective and civilized way to reduce tensions.

Our Middle East policy must be addressed. The peace process must be restarted. The security of the earth depends on new initiatives. Ending the violent conflict between Israel and the Palestinians is not only good for both sides, but for the region and the world.

What are our interests? People are dying. War anywhere is a threat to peace everywhere. The world is tightly bound. Jerusalem is the home of Judaism, Christianity, and Islam; their religious relations run deep. The war divides US and European public opinion and takes resources away from poor nations. Suicide bombers are not likely to be confined to Israel. On September 11, there were attacks in New York and Washington, DC. The war threatens to destabilize the region. A destabilized Middle East changes the world dramatically as we know it. Resources, oil, and energy do matter to the US and Western economy, and those matters need not be a tradeoff for human rights and justice.

The United States and Israel are facing isolation at a time when we need coalition. We are becoming the object of intense hatred and vilification. Many forces are plotting, hoping for our downfall. And yet we choose a unilateral "my way or the highway" philosophy. The arrogance of power is perilous.

We spend half of our foreign aid on two countries, yet we are not getting the desired results of peace, reconciliation, and regional stability. Apparently the resolution is *not* in more money and weapons but in a new policy formula that creates shared security and mutual recognition. Given the bitterness of violence, it requires the right use of our leverage, incentives, and patience, defining our true national interests and making this our chief consideration. It is unreasonable that one-half of our $12 billion foreign-aid budget goes to two countries and the other half goes to the rest of the world. It looks upon Africa—our regional benefactor, our regional source of aid and trade—as an afterthought.

A few days ago at the G8[3] meeting in Canada our government led the way to give the Russians $20 billion to decommission some of its weapons and gave Africa—one-eighth of the human race—a paltry $1 billion, including debt relief. And there was hardly a mention of HIV/AIDS, illiteracy, drinkable water, reciprocal trade, or a plan for development. It looks as if a cross-eyed archer is guiding our foreign policy. While the target of global relief is in one direction, our foreign policy leaders are looking in the wrong direction.

This incomprehensible foreign policy is now having a negative and debilitating effect on our domestic priorities and economy. Since we last met we have gone from a $1.5 trillion ($1,500,000,000,000.00) surplus to a projected deficit of $165 billion ($165,000,000,000.00). The stock market is experiencing an alarming and prolonged decline.

Much of the crisis is attributed to the extreme concentration of capital, which has corrupted and literally melted the democratic process.[4] Checks and balances, separation of powers, transparency have all been purchased on the altar of greed.

Let's look at Enron. The Enron–WorldCom–Global Crossing–Arthur Anderson[5] pattern is much the same. Tragically, much of what they did was legal. Laws had been twisted to protect thievery, greed, and nontransparency. Workers' life savings, college funds for children, health care, retirement plans, and bright futures were all destroyed.

Enron's legal protections masked what was happening so people were misled. For example, let's look at massive tax evasion and the legal rape of the national treasury. Not paying taxes violates the sovereignty of the Treasury Department. Enron used nearly three thousand offshore shell companies to mask their true condition and inflate earnings—tax evasion schemes. They used cook-the-books schemes to avoid paying their fair share of taxes.

These forces used their political power by investing $100 million in the campaign of the president, whose first act was to give back to them half of the budget surplus as incentive for growth. They backed their trucks up to the national treasury, and the guards were removed. When the scandal struck, the president and his advisors' capacity to pursue the violators was compromised by their need to shield themselves. The Department of Justice leadership had to recuse itself for conflict of interest. Vice President Dick Cheney would not cooperate with Congress. Robbers walked away free. The executive branch was compromised and the legislative branch was paralyzed.

When these corporations engage in suspect insider deals and accounting practices they are merely following the bad example of key members of the administration. We need a credible commission on corporate reform and transparency to restore credibility in corporate America.

The Bush administration has utterly failed the country in civil rights. Despite public outcry for election reform and campaign financing Bush has offered no leadership. He opposes affirmative action and wants to "reevaluate" Title IX.[6] Welfare reform under Bush is a race to the bottom. He has appointed anti–civil rights judges and key staff at the Departments of Justice, Education, and elsewhere.

All of the gains of the last fifty years are under attack—being eroded and threatened by this administration. The irony is that while the issue of civil rights is perceived as an issue of black protest because of our historic experience it is the majority whose rights are being diminished amid extreme deference to the very wealthy and corporate misgovernance: the public education of children in Appalachia (white America), rural Alabama or urban Chicago (black America), East Los Angeles (brown America),[7] or on the Pine Ridge Reservation (red America). Public health. Public transportation. The rights of workers, women, and the disabled are all being threatened. There's increased pressure on middle-class workers and taxpayers. It's the *majority* that is under pressure today, not the minority. The "minority" is living in a land of surplus and luxury, splendor and legalized tax evasion. These families wrap themselves in a sense of divine right and privilege, which are antithetical to the promises of a democracy of, by, and for the people. If we are lured only into a race analysis, as pernicious as the skin tax is, we will be slow to see how the North/South gap between the surplus culture of the wealthy minority and the deficit culture of the majority is getting greater.

Against this backdrop, today we are called upon to move from analysis to action. I offer the following program:

1. The Rainbow PUSH Coalition as an organization accepts the burden to build an offensive structure and movement for action for our future. Rainbow PUSH and the NAACP will be doing some strategic work together this fall in defense of civil rights and civil liberties.

2. We will intensify efforts in the One Thousand Churches Con-

nected program (an initiative of the Rainbow PUSH Coalition). One Thousand Churches Connected is not merely to address economic literacy and home ownership—which it has done extremely well—but will teach theology that addresses public policy, corporate ethics, and direct action. The program will be a strong expression not merely of faith but also of works, not just analysis but action. The defining feature of Dr. Martin Luther King Jr.'s work was faith that led to action, to be active where the "rubber hits the road." There was no fear to face the forces of resistance then, and there is no fear now to speak truth to power. When God warned Noah of an impending storm he didn't say, "Teach swimming lessons." He said, build a structure—an ark—that can withstand the storm.

3. The HIV/AIDS crisis is intensifying. Research on prevention and finding a cure continues while the number of cases of infection worldwide increases. Knowledge is power. We will mobilize one million people—beginning *today*—to take the HIV/AIDS test so they can be part of the solution.

4. This coming autumn we will renew our "Count the vote, we will not get over it" drive. We marched in Selma in 1965 for the right to vote. We who honor the right to vote will not get over having our votes discounted, miscounted, and uncounted. There is a moral democratic imperative to protect the vote of each citizen. Election reform will remain at the top of our agenda.

President Bush and Attorney General Ashcroft have a closed-door and no-talk policy toward established civil rights organizations. We have a right to be heard. We are the sons and daughters of the battlefields. We are veterans of foreign wars. Taxpayers in April. And victims of a pattern of hate crimes and domestic terror attacks by officers of the law. We must be heard. And so we will march.

5. We will continue to challenge the federal government for equal protection. Today there is a pattern of domestic terrorism against people of color that involves law enforcement officials. Too many people of color have been killed or seriously injured in

encounters with police officers and sheriff deputies. Federal intervention is necessary to ensure equal protection and personal safety. This requires federal hate crimes legislation and aggressive defense of affirmative action and Title IX.

6. We will build on recent victories to end the death penalty—following on the moratorium issued in Maryland, the Supreme Court ruling banning executions of the mentally retarded, and requiring that juries and not judges make decisions on capital punishment.

7. Education. Last week, Illinois identified 232 failing schools. Most are in poor neighborhoods of African Americans and Latinos. Of the 179 failing schools in Chicago, 178 have predominantly black or Hispanic enrollments. This huge disparity in public education—the achievement gap—is replicated in city after city and state after state, all across the nation. According to today's *Chicago Tribune*, race and poverty define the education achievement gap. Vouchers for a few children do not address those who are left behind. If 10 percent of the children in Cleveland, Ohio, get a $2,200 down payment on a $10,000 private school, what about the other $8,000. What about the 90 percent of students in the public schools left behind? What value does a voucher have to children living in the mountains of Appalachia or in East Los Angeles or rural Iowa or the Pine Ridge Reservation? *All* students demand equity in education, achievement, administration, resources, and opportunity.

8. As we fight for access to capital and business opportunities in counties and states, we must advocate for a ten to twenty day prompt payment. All around the nation, minority businesses tell us that they must wait sixty to ninety days to get paid for services performed. Their businesses are in jeopardy because they are denied the ability to pay their own bills. They cannot buy bread cheaper, and they cannot expect their employees and their creditors to wait sixty to ninety days to be paid. Cities and counties and states must pay promptly for work performed. In the federal government, if you are not paid within ten days, they levy a penalty.

By contrast, cities, counties, and states are three to five months behind in paying for work already done, causing massive bankruptcies of small businesses.

This is the fourth stage of our struggle: the first stage was slavery, the second legal segregation. The third was winning the right to vote. We must be defined today by the fourth stage of our civil rights struggle: our mission is not merely to integrate, become socialized, and sit in public places together, but to integrate access to capital, industry, and technology.

9. Slave era policies. We do know that between eight and twelve million of our foreparents and their descendants were enslaved in the United States from 1619 to 1865. It is estimated that the present value to the US economy from the forced labor of our ancestors is nearly $1.4 trillion. California led the way in requiring the insurance companies to provide the insurance commissioner with information about any life insurance policies it issued on the lives of our foreparents. Other states must do the same. As insurance companies continue to grow and expand, benefiting from the Banking Modernization Act, they must invest in the communities from which they collect premiums. We will be convening state legislators from across the country to develop legislation that ends discriminatory and predatory practices within the financial services industry.

10. Redlining skin tax and predatory economic policies. There is a direct line from slave-era policies to race-based premiums and redlining.[8] Following the first Civil Rights Act in 1868, industrial life policies were introduced to this country beginning the next phase of slavery: economic exploitation. For decades, insurance companies used dual mortality tables based on race to justify charging higher premiums to black citizens for virtually worthless polices. Thousands of African Americans wanting to pass on some form of wealth to their families, just as the majority population does, were sold inferior insurance products at higher rates. Currently over seventy corporations are under investigation, and there are nearly twenty lawsuits; yet the majority of citizens remain

unaware of this systematic use of racism to exploit hard-working parents, grandparents, ministers, and ordinary people merely wanting to leave behind something more than just cherished memories.

Today I call on us to act to honor the tradition and methodologies of those who got us to this stage of our struggle for "a more perfect Union" and a more peaceful world. We left on our journey some years ago. We've not yet reached the Promised Land. Moses could not stop in the middle of the Red Sea. The waters would have closed in on him. Pharaoh's army would have caught him.

Joshua could not march around the walls of Jericho for half a week silently. He had to march the whole week and blow the trumpets. Daniel could not fear the lions in the den. He had the trust of God, who had locked their jaws and turned their growl into music. Jesus could not fear Herod. He had to march on Palm Sunday and know there was resurrection power beyond the grave.

Gandhi had to act. Mandela had to act. Dr. King had to march. Dr. King suffered and sacrificed. We must honor that tradition. We must use the pitter-patter of our marching feet and go forward. Take our case to the Department of Justice. Take our case to the White House. Take our case to the ballot box this fall. Take our case to Wall Street. Take our case to the Middle East. Take our case to Africa. Take our case to the Caribbean.

And with the full assurance that if we are right, God will help fight our battle. I know the midnight hour is dark. But joy cometh in the morning because trouble will not last always. We need to have the full assurance that God did not bring us this far to leave us now. So we march for healing and hope. God will forgive our sins and heal our land.

Keep hope alive.

10

Beating Swords into Plowshares

**International Peace Foundation
Bangkok, Thailand
November 2003**

Thank you for inviting me here today, to your beautiful country. It is an honor to be with you. Let us start with a moment of prayer, a moment of reconciliation, a moment of nonviolence, and a moment of peace.

Fill your heads with visions of Dr. King and Gandhi; fill your hearts with thoughts of peace and nonviolence. Remember the words of the prophet Isaiah:

> And He shall judge among the nations, and shall rebuke many people: and they shall beat their swords into plowshares, and their spears into pruning hooks; nation shall not lift up sword against nation, neither shall they learn war any more. (Isaiah 2:4)

The Global Peace Movement

Last February 15th, I had the privilege of speaking in London to what may have been the largest antiwar rally in history, and certainly one of the highlights of the largest one-day global demonstration for peace in world history.

Millions of people, all over the world, all over Europe, on both coasts in the United States, and in more than 600 sites around the globe, took to the streets to say no to an American preemptive military strike on Iraq. Literally millions and millions of people, many of them young people, put their bodies in the path of the war machine. Two million in London; 500,000 in Berlin; 250,000 in Paris; two million in Rome; a million in Madrid, plus another million in Barcelona; 10,000 in the Canary Islands; 50,000 in Glasgow; half a million in New York, plus another quarter of a million in San Francisco. Hundreds of thousands more in Amsterdam, Athens, Hong Kong, and Bangkok.

On that day a new global peace movement was born. All over the world on February 15th, the people rose up for peace. It is our job to keep that spirit alive in the months and years to come.

Dr. King's Last Birthday

As I stood before that crowd in London I thought back to Dr. Martin Luther King Jr. When I was young I had the honor of serving with Dr. King, one of the greatest peacemakers who ever lived. I was with him on his last birthday. Let me share with you how he spent that day, his thirty-ninth birthday, January 15, 1968.

We met together to make plans for a three-point agenda:

- to pull together a multiracial coalition with a commitment to mass action, to fight a war on poverty in the United States;
- to make sure civil rights laws were enforced and justice was done; and
- to end the war in Vietnam, choosing containment and negotiation over endless bombing and confrontation, to give peace a chance.

We chose minds over missiles. We chose coexistence over coannihilation. We chose negotiation over confrontation and intimidation.

I remembered that last birthday as I spoke in Hyde Park in London. And so I appealed to the huge crowd—and to Britain's prime minister Tony Blair—to help stop the war with Iraq before it started. To choose life over death, hope and healing over hurt and hostility.

President Bush drew a line in the sand. The president spoke of evil, of mushroom clouds, of terrorists; I spoke of peace. But it is not enough to choose sides—we must reconcile sides because there are rarely winners during wartime. Young soldiers and civilians kill and are killed. Cities and ancient relics are destroyed. Water is made unclean, the air is polluted, disease and decay spread.

There is no future, no growth, and no prosperity for the average person in that equation. Instead we must find a way to make lions lie down with lambs.

Retaliation or Reconciliation

When the United States, the world's superpower, searches for victory or retaliation rather than reconciliation, it ignores the consequences and global repercussions. It ignores the tragedy inflicted on the Iraqi people, defenseless in their homes. And it ignores the likelihood of "blowback," smaller nations circling back later to inflict more pain on our own people, citizens of the superpower.

Invading Iraq in March 2003 began the battle, but it did not end the terror. And filling the air with threatening rhetoric from America's old Wild West and Hollywood movies only fanned the flames of fear and hatred and violence and reaction. The rhetorical war is a psychological war that has already created ominous tension around the world. President Bush bragged about raining down, from the heavens, a military armada of "shock and awe" on the Iraqi people. Such bullying talk has clouded the skies of reconciliation and justice.

After 9/11 the world stood on America's side. People were ready to fight the Taliban because the whole world understood that they had enabled al-Qaeda to attack us. But only two years later, most of the world has moved away from the United States. Most of the world does not put Iraq on the same team as al-Qaeda. Saddam

Hussein was not liked, but he was also not feared nearly as much as al-Qaeda.

Then there is North Korea, desperate, destitute, and dangerous.

And there is the ongoing crisis between Israel and the Palestinians, where the supposed road map for peace now lies in tatters.

But the administration fast-forwarded past all three of these very real crises—al-Qaeda's survival, the North Korean nuclear arsenal, and the escalating cycle of violence between Israel and the Palestinians—to invade and occupy Iraq.

The world did not believe us when we said that the threat from Iraq was imminent, and so far the administration's "proofs" have been totally unconvincing. The world saw Iraq as trapped in a glass jar, contained for the past twelve years, subject to no-fly zones, daily bombings, U-2 and spy-drone over-flights. Iraq was contained, weaker than ever, no threat to its neighbors unless attacked. And most important, Iraq had dismantled its weapons of mass destruction.

The world has never believed that suddenly the Bush administration was intensely interested in the liberation of the Iraqi people. The world knows that we sold Hussein much of the arsenal he used to fight Iran, to gas the Kurds, to subjugate his own people. As one comedian put it, the reason we knew Iraq once had weapons of mass destruction was because we had the receipts.

The world believed that this war was about oil, not terrorism; about payback, not regime change; about destroying Saddam Hussein rather than destroying weapons of mass destruction; about empire, not democracy.

And leading figures in all religions have made it crystal clear that there was no moral foundation for a US war in Iraq for these reasons. We had no basis in Christian or other theologies to fight a war to secure our right to drive big cars and bigger trucks with stolen Iraqi oil.

In the arrogance to rush to war, the hawks underestimated the perils, the price, and the pain. To rush to war without fully counting the moral and physical and fiscal risks was arrogant; and arrogance precedes the fall. I made this point before the war ever started; I make it again now, when new crises loom while old ones linger unresolved.

The truth is that, even for a superpower, while the war may be short, the cycle of violence will go on. An eye for an eye and a tooth for a tooth leaves everyone blind and eating mush. When a superpower invades a smaller country, global terrorism spreads. Nevertheless, as I reminded the marchers in London last February, as a global peace movement we must not blindly rush toward unconditional peace without justice. We all know the rule—no justice, no peace.

Peace without security and accountability is naïve; it is just the absence of conflict—it is not the presence of justice. No one can fruitfully search for victory in this conflict—there is another level. We must not choose sides; we must choose reconciliation; we must choose coexistence over coannihilation; mutual development over mutual destruction.

An Appeal to Saddam Hussein

Twelve years ago, armed only with my faith and the logic of choosing life over death, I took the risk of talking to President Saddam Hussein of Iraq, and the lives of six hundred hostages were saved. I brought them out of Baghdad, back to their homes in Britain, France, Canada, and the United States. I took the risk of talking to Hussein and it worked.

So before the war started last winter I wrote an open letter to Hussein, asking him to cooperate fully with the United Nations inspectors, to allow them to search Iraq's weapons' capabilities. I pointed out that this was the only way to save the women and children of Baghdad. My point was that secrecy would no longer protect him; only transparency could possibly avert war.

In England I also appealed to Prime Minister Tony Blair to please take a step back from this war. I reminded him that the archbishop of Canterbury, the pope, Desmond Tutu (the emeritus archbishop of Cape Town, South Africa), and Nelson Mandela (a moral conscience of the world) all said the war was wrong, that it was immoral. I pointed out that this war would be his legacy and that surely that is not what he most wanted to be remembered for.

I appealed to Tony Blair to use his incredible political talents, his intelligence, and his undeniable charm to reach out to Iraq. I suggested that Prime Minister Blair put his stamp of approval on an "Eminent Persons Commission" empowered by UN Secretary General Kofi Annan and the United Nations (a commission perhaps headed by Nelson Mandela), to go to Baghdad and convince Saddam Hussein that open inspections and transparency were the answer. Tony Blair had the leverage back in February to make such an Eminent Persons Commission possible and to avoid war while the inspectors and perhaps UN peacekeepers pulled us back from the brink of war.

Instead, Tony Blair stayed on the course of war. I believe history will be unkind to that decision. Certainly it has hurt his poll numbers, his party, and his legacy. Just to try every avenue, I even appealed to President Bush, who has told us all many times that Jesus changed his heart, that Jesus, the Prince of Peace, saved him from his youthful mistakes and lack of direction.

Well what would Jesus have done about Iraq? As a preacher, as a student of the Bible, as a lifelong Christian, I cannot accept that Jesus's answer to the supposed weapons-of-mass-destruction crisis would have been to launch missiles on the women and children of Baghdad. That is not the Jesus I know in my heart. And I am presumptuous enough to suggest that most other religious leaders would agree with me. Certainly Dr. King would; Gandhi would.

The Moral Center

One of the big lessons that Dr. King taught me, that Mahatma Gandhi taught us all, is that times of crisis can also be times of opportunity. Points of pain can turn into chances for change. At a time of unnecessary war a global peace movement is reborn. That is one reason why I often travel to points of pain. I believe peace is worth the risk, so I try when others say it is hopeless.

At a time of crisis I went to Syria in 1983—I tried, and a downed American airman was freed.[1] I went to Cuba in 1984 and took Castro to church—we talked and the result was freed prisoners. I went to Iraq in 1990 before the first Gulf War, when the bombs were about to fall, and got Saddam Hussein to agree that he should free a planeload of hostages. I even went to Serbia in 1999 and got Slobodan Milosevic to free three captured soldiers—I tried and they all got to go home.

Points of pain are often chances for change. The key to transformation, however, is that those oppressed must remain committed to nonviolence, redemption, and reconciliation. The goal is not that the lambs overthrow the lions. The goal is that lions and lambs reconcile and work out a new arrangement where everyone prospers. In the American South, the fire hoses and vicious police dogs of Sheriff Bull Connor in Birmingham led to the Civil Rights Act of 1964. And now we have a New South, where both whites and blacks are better off.

The March 7, 1965, head-beatings of civil rights marchers in Selma, Alabama—as they attempted to cross a bridge to challenge Governor George Wallace—those beatings led directly to America's Voting Rights Act of 1965. And now we have a broader, more inclusive Democratic Party that has transcended its segregationist past.

When Gandhi marched to the sea with his masses of the scorned and dispossessed, suddenly colonialism became untouchable. Suddenly democracy in India became not just possible but likely. Suddenly the downtrodden were elevated to a new level of dignity.

When women suffragists chained themselves to the railings of the prime minister's front door in London in 1908, sexism crumbled and women won the right to vote. And now women lead nations, head corporations, run a full-court fast break in basketball, organize new unions, and preach in our churches.

When workers sat down in the automobile factories in the

1930s, the corporations trembled and trade unions were born. And an American middle class was created that helped lead the United States to decades of unimagined prosperity.

Dr. King and Gandhi recognized that politics could be redefined, society turned inside out and upside down, if people—poor people—working people—and especially young people—acted together, non-violently, on behalf of the moral center.

At certain times, history pauses at the crossroad.

At certain times, "soul force" can overcome armies, topple tyrants, and knock down walls.

At certain times, a prisoner on Robben Island becomes a prophet for the whole world, and apartheid is broken. Nelson Mandela spent twenty-seven years in jail but hung on long enough to free his jailer; together, we can change history.[2]

At certain times, polar opposites can be reconciled, and societies can be redeemed.

With the rise of a global peace movement, this may be such a time.

A Better World Is Possible

During the Cold War we used to say that the oppressed peoples of Eastern Europe were denied a voice. They were not allowed to speak. Today in our Western democracies the people are speaking with their feet. As millions marched in Europe and the United States, the question became—will their leaders listen? The people are speaking—would they be heard?

One of the great theological principles is fairness. The concept of balance is the Golden Rule—to do unto others as we wish others to do unto us. In the old stories of the Bible the great cities were in balance, their height and breadth in proportion to each other.

But today's world is not in balance.

Today we have shining cities on the hill with technological prowess and massive wealth and unimaginable creature comforts. That is one-sixth of the world, what I call the "surplus" cultures, the cultures of privilege. And then we have the "deficit" cultures, the cultures of pain, five-sixths of the world.

Until we bring the world into balance, until we drain the swamps of poverty and disease and inequality which are the breeding grounds of terrorist recruiting, until we universalize the Golden Rule among nations—until then, we will not have peace. We will not have justice. We will not live up to the moral imperatives to feed the hungry, to heal the sick, to shelter the refugee.

We can do better than guided missiles and misguided morals.

We can do better than policies that excite the surplus cultures but depress or alienate the deficit cultures.

We can do better than letting 365,000 children die every single day from what the United Nations calls "conditions of starvation."

Our religions, our morality, our deepest values call on us to do better than this world of growing inequality where "the richest fifth of the world's people consume 86 percent of all goods and services while the poorest fifth are left with just over 1 percent." The United Nations Human Development Report of 1999 also reported that "the income gap between the fifth of the world's people living in the richest countries and the fifth in the poorest doubled from 1960 to 1990, from 30-to-1 to 60-to-1. By 1998 it had jumped again with the gap widening to an astonishing 78 to 1."

We can do better than our current habit of ignoring the three billion people around the globe who try to scrape by on less than two dollars per day. We can do better than ignoring the obvious fact that global warming is now endangering future generations. We could commit to rebuilding our world. My nation is the world's number-one arms dealer, and it pains me to say so.

We could waste less on weapons of war and mass destruction and spend more on growing food, cleaning the air and the water, curing the age-old diseases that still torment the poor, fighting HIV/AIDS in Africa and Asia and Latin America and all around the world, ending child labor, ending childhood sex exploitation, inventing and distributing renewable energy technologies, and building schools for our children.

A better world is still possible.

But to get there we will have to find leaders willing to suggest policies that excite the deficit cultures while upsetting many in the surplus cultures. From global warming to the role of international institutions, to fairness in global trade, to lifting the yoke of debt on the poorer nations, the United States finds itself on the side of the privileged—and the rest of the world understands it better than we do.

We have come back full circle to a profound point that Dr. King made on April 4, 1967, when he spoke out against the US role in the Vietnam War at New York's Riverside Church.

Dr. King taught "we must rapidly begin the shift from a thing-oriented society to a person-oriented society. When machines and computers, profit motives and property rights, are considered more important than people, the giant triplets of racism, extreme materialism, and militarism are incapable of being conquered."

In that speech, Dr. King went on:

> A true revolution of values will soon cause us to question the fairness and justice of many of our past and present policies. . . . A true revolution of values will soon look uneasily on the glaring contrast of poverty and wealth. . . . A genuine revolution of values means in the final analysis that our loyalties must become ecumenical rather than sectional. Every nation must develop an overriding loyalty to mankind as a whole in order to preserve the best in their individual societies. . . . We can no longer afford to worship the god of hate or bow before the altar of retaliation. . . . We still have a choice today: non-violent coexistence or violent co-annihilation. . . . We must find new ways to speak for peace . . . and justice throughout the developing world.[3]

A New Foreign Policy

With a true revolution in values, American foreign policy would not wander so far from our fundamental values. When I ran for president in 1988 I articulated five principles for a new American foreign policy: respect for international law; human rights; self-determination; economic justice; consistency—measuring by one yardstick.

I believed then and I believe now that all nations must play by one set of rules. The fact that the United States is strong enough to ignore other nations, at least in the short term, is not the same as saying it makes sense to do so, or that it is somehow moral to bully them, intimidate them, or bribe them into supporting our unilateral decisions.

The destruction and debasement of international institutions, the abandonment of international treaties, the tough talk about other nations, even our longtime allies like France and Germany— this is not good policy, and it is extremely damaging over the long term.

After all, the world is a rainbow of people. Even the US population is becoming more diverse with each passing year.

Remember that when President Bush and Prime Minister Blair get together to talk about Iraq it's a minority meeting. They represent only 5 percent of the world, one out of every twenty people. As all of you know, half the world lives in Asia, with half of them in China. A billion people live in India next door to their foe Pakistan. And both are armed with weapons of mass destruction. One-eighth of the world lives in Africa, one-fourth of them in Nigeria, where HIV/AIDS, hunger, and disease are devastating the continent. The United States is not even a majority in its own hemisphere, where more people speak Spanish than English, and almost as many people speak Portuguese.

Here's a fact that you understand, but most Americans do not realize: most people in the world are black, brown, yellow, young, female, non-Christian, and don't speak English.

We must learn to live together. If, as moral human beings, we want to end violence in the world, unilateralism is a dead end. Multilateralism is a necessity, with development and not destruction. The United States must once again work hand in hand with its allies, with developing nations, with the United Nations. Cooperation is the watchword, not contempt.

The wealth of the world must be shared more fairly. The lost sheep of which Jesus spoke must be found, and fed, and healed. The bread and fishes that Jesus shared with the multitudes must now be shared with Quito as well as Cleveland, Lagos as well as Los Angeles, Bangkok as well as Baltimore.

A better world is still possible.

Lions and Lambs

There will be no peace until lions and lambs lie down together. Until the strong and the weak mutually agree to reconcile. But what would make an arrogant and powerful lion agree to lie down with a lamb? And what would make a weak and defenseless lamb agree to trust a lion long enough to lie still?

Only one thing—they have mutual interests. Coalitions of unlikely partners are built on mutual interests, common ground. Both the lion and the lamb will be destroyed if the forests are set on fire. Both lions and lambs will perish if the air is warmed too much, and the ice caps melt, and the oceans wash up over our islands and shorelines, and the ecology of the jungle and the farm are forever altered.

Neither a lion nor a lamb can exist while drinking polluted waters. Neither a lion nor a lamb can survive a smart bomb—or, for that matter, a fundamentalist fanatic armed with a box cutter or a suicide bomb.

Common ground leads to coalition. Talking together and working together and prospering together lead to reconciliation. The Golden Rule has not been repealed—do unto others as ye would have others do unto you. This rule works for nations as well as for neighbors.

Dr. King's lesson still lives: "The arc of history is long, but it bends toward justice." Spirit and faith will always be tested; but faith can move mountains. It's dark but the morning comes.

Faith helped Moses march out of Egypt and across the Red Sea.
Faith helped Joshua bring the walls tumbling down.
Faith helped Jesus turn crucifixion into resurrection.
Faith kept Mandela alive long enough to liberate his own jailer.
Someday swords will be beaten into plowshares.
Someday lions will lie down with lambs.
Someday justice will roll down like waters, and righteousness like a mighty stream.

11

The Challenge to Build
a More Perfect Union

**Rainbow PUSH Annual Convention
Chicago, Illinois
June 28, 2004**

Today as we meet here with the Rainbow PUSH family, we reflect on the milestones of our civil rights history: fifty years since *Brown v. Board of Education*; nearly forty years since the Voting Rights Act and the Selma March, forty since Birmingham and the 1964 Civil Rights Act; twenty years since our historic run for the presidency in 1984.

Our history is full of twists and turns and winding roads, but history as we know it always bends toward justice. But the past few years there has been a different wind blowing. Walmart, the largest company in the world, pushed down wages and health care benefits, and now it is the target of a major discrimination lawsuit filed by women workers. It's a sign of the times.

The merger of JP Morgan Chase and Bank One, a $60 billion merger, with $100 million in transaction fees going to financial services and law firms but not a single black company involved in the deal. It's a sign of the times.

Bush's war of choice in Iraq based on lies and distortions, with $200 billion spent, is creating more enemies than allies, with soldiers and citizens dying each day and no end in sight. It's a sign of the times.

A record surplus in 2000 turned into record deficits and three million jobs lost. Tax breaks for the wealthy and job cuts for working families. A recovery with jobs paying less with fewer benefits. It's a sign of the times.

More black men in prison than in college in every state; states turning the prison industrial complex into booming private industries with blacks once again the commodity. It's a sign of the times.

An administration that has not met one time with civil rights organizations or labor in three years and a Justice Department with a closed door policy and a closed ear to civil rights. It's a sign of the times.

I tell you today my friends we need a change. We need new leadership and a new direction. The stakes in this November's US presidential election have never been higher.

What Do We Want?

I am convinced that we must return to our roots to find our power and protect our interests. But first we must define *what* we want.

The Bible says where there is no vision the people perish. It further says a leader should not blow a trumpet with an uncertain sound. It is making the case for a mission statement. The ideological right in control of our nation knows what it wants.

The right wing fights for a series of constitutional amendments. They intend to have their ideology protected by the highest law in the land. They intend to push the ideology of the Confederacy— states' rights—and continue to challenge the vision of "a more perfect Union."

They have a blind obsession with the Second Amendment's right to bear arms, and the National Rifle Association wants to remove the ban on assault weapons, AK-47s and Uzis, in September during a time of national security alert. They want a constitutional amendment to ban flag burning. They want a constitutional amendment to ban gay marriage. They want a balanced budget amendment—it only appears elsewhere in the Confederate Constitution—requiring three-fourths of the Congress to raise taxes. They focus on using their power to get laws that protect their vision of America no matter who the leader is in a certain season.

In this competing vision of America we choose the Union over the Confederacy. We choose a simple but comprehensive plan to make America "a more perfect Union." *What do we want?*

At the center of our new progressive agenda is the passage of a constitutional amendment that guarantees the individual right to vote, which should be part of the Democratic Party platform. Today we merely have a *states'* right to vote, where fifty state elections with odd and uneven machinery left two million votes—and one million black votes—discounted in the *Al Gore v. George W. Bush* 2000 presidential election. In Florida, 179,000 votes were not counted at all; 54 percent of those were black.

Let me say that one more time. In 2000 there were two million votes that went *uncounted*—not just in Florida but around the country and right here in Cook County, Illinois. And one million uncounted black votes. The ballots "spoiled" not because of a lack of refrigeration; they were just locked out of the count.

What do we want? We want an amendment to the Constitution to guarantee workers the right to organize without interference. We want a Department of Labor and National Labor Relations Board that enforces the law. We want to make health care a human right—a constitutional amendment to guarantee equal high quality health care for every individual American.

What do we want? We want an amendment to the Constitution to guarantee equal, high-quality public education for every American, whether in Appalachia, Alabama, California, or New York. We need environmental protection, a constitutional right to breathe free—with drinkable water not polluted by corporate greed and waste.

Workers deserve an even playing field, just as athletes have in the Olympics. We will do well in Athens, Greece, because the field is even, the rules are public, the goals are clear, and the refs are fair. When Shaq O'Neil plays Yao Ming in the National Basketball Association (NBA), it's a fair contest because the playing field is even.

Progressive Southern Strategy "Based on the Base"

This democratic agenda is the unfinished business of the civil rights movement. Not "back in the civil rights days" but *today*. But what's different today is that *we have the power*; we have the ability to control our own destiny.

We need a progressive Southern strategy based on our strength and base. Many pundits and politicians no longer see the importance of the South. President Bush is depending on the conservative South to return him to office. But the South, I tell you, is unnaturally conservative. The South is the poorest region in our nation and, therefore, has the least to conserve.

Four decades after the 1965 Selma March there are still eight to ten million African Americans who are not registered to vote: 936,000 unregistered in New York; 600,000 unregistered in Georgia; 550,000 in Texas; 530,000 in North Carolina; 380,000 unregistered in Illinois; 500,000 in New Jersey; 475,000 in Virginia; in Florida, 600,000 unregistered; 400,000 in Mississippi; 300,000 in South Carolina; and 300,000 unregistered in Louisiana. There are nearly a million in New York and 215,000 in Alabama. In South Carolina's last major election 288,000 African Americans did not vote, and only 278,000 did. More blacks didn't vote than did. And Democrats lost that race by 40,000 votes. And there are still 300,000 unregistered voters in that state.

Last year in Louisiana, Mary Landrieu won her seat in the US Senate on the strength of the black vote led by State Senator Cleo Fields. Even though the right wing's national apparatus focused solely on this race and it was the only one to take place on that day, progressive forces achieved a victory. At first Landrieu started with a "drive-by campaign," waving at our community but not engaging. So Cleo put out a bumper sticker saying, "Don't respect us, then don't expect us." We met with Senator Landrieu and got an understanding; the conflict was resolved and Landrieu won.

In the last campaign 75,000 jobs were lost, drowned out by the race issue in South Carolina. In Alabama there are 250,000 blacks still unregistered; the last governor won by just 10,000 votes.

That's why I make the case for registering and empowering the black vote, and for winning back the nation on a progressive Southern strategy "based on our base." The key to liberating the nation is the South. The key to liberating the South is the black vote. The formula is straight and simple: register new black and Latino voters; strengthen their alliance with labor; focus a message of jobs, health care, and shared economic security; and increase voter turnout. That was our strategy when I ran for president of the United States in 1984 and 1988, bottom-up, grass-roots mobilization and organizing.

Expand the Center

There is a prevailing political equation: there's 40 percent to the right, 40 percent to the left, and 20 percent in the center. Parties compete for the center "swing vote." But this equation is not static. It must change. Activism, registration, and participation can expand both the moral and the political center.

Lest we forget, slavery lasted 246 years. Abolition was in the moral center but not in the political center. We could not legally vote and we were not in the political center. For the 89 years to end Jim Crow and win civil rights we were outside of the political center but in the moral center. In the 1960 Democratic Party's National Convention that nominated then-Massachusetts senator John F. Kennedy to head their presidential ticket, the civil rights agenda was outside of the political center. The 1964 convention in Atlantic City and the movement to seat the Mississippi Freedom Democratic Party was outside of the political center.[1]

But the morally centered sit-ins, protests, and activism of the 1960s expanded the political center. The morally centered 1965 Voting Rights Act, the march from Selma, and the antiwar movement expanded the political center.

But our base is sometimes dismissed as "not being in the center," and we are pushed to the margins. But if we are energized around morally just issues we can change the entire equation. In our 1984 presidential campaign we registered two million new voters formerly in the margins. We expanded the center and returned the Senate Democrats to power and control of the US Senate in 1986. Our 1988 presidential campaign in 1990 brought us Dave Dinkins, the first black elected mayor of New York City. In 1989 Virginia governor Doug Wilder became first black person elected governor anywhere in the United States since Reconstruction and countless others who became empowered and elected to offices in towns, cities, counties, and states across the nation. Remember George H. W. Bush and Robert Dole got more white votes combined in their 1988 Republican presidential primary campaigns than Bill Clinton; but Clinton got more white, black, brown, and Asian votes in the1992 general presidential election than they did, and he won.

Those in the margins are the key to our destiny of a one-big-tent America—challenging right-wing control of our country. The dream of a one-big-tent America is within reach. This was the challenge of our political leaders and parties, to expand the center and be inclusive when I ran for president of the United States in 1984 and 1988. And at the 1984 Democratic National Convention, I said in San Francisco:

> This is not a perfect party. We are not a perfect people. Yet, we are called to a perfect mission. Our mission: to feed the hungry; to clothe the naked; to house the homeless; to teach the illiterate; to provide jobs for the jobless; and to choose the human race over the nuclear race. We are gathered here to expand, unify, direct, and inspire our nation to fulfill this

mission . . . to motivate, register, and mobilize the desperate, the damned, the disinherited, the disrespected, and the despised. They are restless and seek relief. They have voted in record numbers. We have invested our faith, hope, and trust that they have in us. Now parties and candidates must send them a signal that we care.

A Program of Action

Today, just as true as it was twenty years ago in San Francisco, we issue a call of conscience, redemption, expansion, healing, and unity. We can win. Leadership can part the waters and lead our nation in the direction of the Promised Land. Leadership can lift the boats stuck at the bottom. We can win.

So where do we go from here?

First, fighting the Walmart factor undermining our economy and national health. We beat Walmart in Inglewood, California, and cities across America, and unions around the nation are waging the battle against the "Walmartization" of the economy—cheap wages at home and slave wages abroad; depressing health care and worker benefits; violating labor law.

Walmart, with its right-to-work ideology suppressing wages and offering few benefits, was able to come to Chicago, a union town, in part because they went across the South untouched and unchallenged.

Walmart is part of the globalization of capital. But if you globalize capital you must globalize labor rights, environmental rights, women's and children's rights. The right to affordable medicine and clean drinkable water is everyone's right across this earth.

Walmart now faces a huge sex discrimination suit. In matters of race and trade exploitation they are just as vulnerable. If we fight to even the playing field for the American worker and see the necessity of our black-brown-white working class coalition we will *win* and deserve to win.

Second, let's return to white, working-class Appalachia. We just took a tour through Appalachia June 6–9 with Cecil Roberts of the UMWA (the United Mine Workers of America), AFSCME (American Federation of State, Council, and Municipal Employees), and CBTU (Coalition of Black Trade Unionists), steel workers, bricklayers, and electrical workers. I stayed in the homes of proud unemployed miners and pensioners with black lung disease who are in a state of increasing desperation.

Why Appalachia? It allows us to deracialize the debate—contrary to stereotypes, most poor people are not black or brown, they are white, female, young, and underserved. They too must be under one big tent of protection. So we put the agenda of reputable working poor people in the national equation. Coal miners who energize the nation, steel workers who built the nation, teachers who teach the nation, bus drivers who transport the nation. What did we find? Thirty-two steel mills have been closed. A coal miner dies every six hours of black lung disease. Children take two-and-a-half-hour bus rides to school each way to schools built in the 1930s. Hundreds of thousands of jobs lost.

We are going back to Appalachia on Labor Day weekend. We must never surrender that territory of working poor people again. If we can cut the military budget without cutting our defense— and we can—we can use that money to rebuild bridges and put steel workers back to work, use that money and provide jobs for our cities, and use that money to build schools and pay teachers and educate our children and build hospitals and train doctors and train nurses; the whole nation will come running to us.

Third, we're going back to Florida in July, the scene of the 2000 crime where our votes were not counted in the presidential race, to convene our leadership to strategize on protecting and mobilizing the vote. We will go to the Democratic Convention in Boston, where Rainbow delegates and leaders will reunite and then go on to protest in New York in August. From Florida to Louisiana we will travel the South to mobilize our base, expand the center, and win in November. In 2000, a voter calamity of enormous proportions occurred. This time we will be prepared to protect our vote and make sure that every vote is counted. This November we will remember!

We must explore building a structure that will allow us to register voters, deliver for voters, and negotiate for their interests. All too often these voters are not under the tent. They are not in the center. They are outside. Their interests—civil rights, civil liberties, peace, and fair-trade policy—are not a part of the discussion. We must build a vehicle to get them to the table for negotiation and resolution.

Fourth, we must review our covenant with corporate America and move the equation from "diversity" to equity and parity. Generational inheritances have left distributorships, franchises, land, and capital in the hands of the few and left us fundamentally outside of the equation. Excellence and effort matter to us, but inheritance and access to capital matter even more.

John Deere was founded in 1837, twenty-seven years before slavery ended. Yet even today John Deere does not have a single African American–owned franchise. They may have some diversity in their employees, but *no inclusion* in their ownership/franchise base. This same pattern holds true in the food and beverage industry, the fast food industry, auto dealerships—we do not have an equitable fair share. And we must *redefine* this relationship.

Fifth, prison-sentencing guidelines are now being exposed as being too harsh and too rigid with no effect on the crime rate. "Crime and Time" don't correspond; it only fills our prisons with youth, mainly black and brown.

Sixth, we will challenge the predatory, exorbitant, phone service fees charged to inmates by states, counties, and sheriff's departments who control the prison telephone systems. They have a monopoly. In Louisiana, for example, the state brings in $6 million a year from prison-based telephone services.

Seventh, we will challenge predatory practices in the financial services, insurance, auto, and other industries. We continue to work harder—for less. Pay more—for less. Even our college degrees are worth less. We live under stress and don't live as long.

Clear Choices

I would make this case today: we value a victory in November. We the people can win. We must reject this Hollywood notion of organized expressions of congeniality and rich young rulers who dress casually and search for a phrase or two to identify with the common people. Leadership must be about values and priorities. The Bible warns us to beware of wolves in sheep's clothing that come smiling but have violent appetites. It warns us against a bush that is a barren victory that has leaves but not fruit. Let's look at our choices, our alternatives, and not be deceived.

1. Iraq: The United States is spinning into global isolation. The United States is losing moral authority and credibility in the world, choosing discredited Ahmad Chalabi and some Iraqi exiles over Hans Blix of the United Nations and the advice of our friends in Germany and France.[2] It was wrong to abuse presidential power and mislead the nation with lies and distortions on Iraq. Clear choices.

2. We have lost nearly nine hundred lives of the poor and the young, $200 billion in costs and rising. We have a plan to rebuild Iraq's infrastructure but not for America. We are creating more enemies than allies. We are sinking in the sand. We need an administration that shifts from a rhythm of preemptive strike, invasion, occupation, and conquest . . . to coalition, partnerships, and withdrawal. Clear choices.

3. And today's supposed "transfer of power" in Iraq does nothing to change this reality. This new Leadership Council is not derived from the people. The CIA appoints it with little more than a steering committee called a governing council. The masses are being led by the clerics, and the United States is still controlling the military and the beneficiaries of economic spoils. It does little to change reality on the ground. Our troops are still in grave danger without adequate resources or a clear mission.

We went into Iraq virtually alone; Bush's pride will not allow a change from a failed course. We need new beginnings. You have clear choices in November.

4. Bush's tax cut is top down rather than reinvest bottom up, and it is bankrupting the nation. We have gone from a projected $5.8 trillion surplus, to a $600 billion deficit and sinking, potentially bankrupting Social Security along the way. Clear choices.

5. A tax cut for the top 1 percent that has kicked 300,000 poor children out of their after-school programs, 23,000 uniformed officers off the street and 140,000 unemployed workers out of their job training programs. Clear choices.

6. An administration and Justice Department with a closed door policy to labor and civil rights and a hostile agenda violating civil liberties. Clear choices.

7. An administration that appoints judges who are antilabor and anti–civil rights. One day it puts up a picture of Dr. King in the White House, and the next day it sends its lawyers to try to kill affirmative action. One day it lays a wreath at Dr. King's gravesite, and the next day it appoints right-wing Charles W. Pickering as a judge on the federal bench in Mississippi. Clear choices.

One side sees America through a keyhole and sees about 1 percent; another side sees America through an open door and sees the rest of us.

The choice is not about "anybody but this administration"; it's about an alternative to its point of view. We have clear choices in November, and you have the right and power to determine the direction of our nation.

Twenty Years since the Rainbow Coalition 1984 Campaign: Changing the Equation

In all of this I reflect on the twenty years since our Rainbow Coalition run for the presidency in 1984. We must build an independent voter infrastructure to register, deliver voters, expand the center, and pass a constitutional amendment affirming the federal individual right to vote.

Many voters never show up because their issues are not addressed and there is no promise of delivery. Blind patriotism does not motivate them to fight for a promise never made or seldom kept.

We are often reminded that we live in a great nation—and we do. But it can be greater still. Rainbow PUSH is mandating a new definition of greatness. We must not measure greatness from the mansion down but from the manger up. Jesus said that we should not be judged by the bark we wear but by the fruit that we bear. Jesus said that we must measure greatness by how we treat the least of these.

If we lift up a program to feed the hungry, they'll come running; if we lift up a program to study war no more, our youth will come running; if we lift up a program Reinvest in America and Put America Back to Work, and an alternative to welfare and despair, they will come working.

The black vote can change the equation. If energized, it can initiate change and change the nation. In spite of the odds and our history what is phenomenal today is that the black vote can determine its destiny, determine the destiny of labor, determine the direction of the parties, the courts, economic policy, Africa, and global affairs. In the face of oppression the only question is, "How do we respond?" We can resist and empower or internalize our pain and accept our place in the system's low expectations of us.

We choose to fight back; create new space for a new place in our nation's drive to become "a more perfect Union." I would argue that the oppressor is not likely to change its profitable ways. The burden is on us, the oppressed, to initiate, fight for, and demand change. We may not be responsible for being down, but we must be responsible for getting up. Those behind and even shackled must run faster and be more determined.

Today, with the power we have earned over the last fifty years through struggles and martyrdom we must fight self-destructive tendencies and cynicism. We must choose the high road of hope and avoid the low road of high-risk behavior. If we maximize and use our strength and power and vote to our fullest and build coalitions, we can beat the odds, negating cynics, and become dream makers with the power to revive our will to nonnegotiable dignity.

We Can Win

As we hold our convention this week we are ready to go back across this nation—to Florida, to Boston, New York, Louisiana, to Michigan and Wisconsin, all across the nation. Today I leave you with the same words I spoke at the Democratic National Convention in San Francisco, July 17, 1984.

> We leave this place looking for the sunny side because there's a brighter side somewhere. I'm more convinced than ever that we can win. We will vault up the rough side of the mountain. We can win. I just want young America to do me one favor, just one favor. Exercise the right to dream. You must face reality—that which is.
>
> But then dream of a reality that ought to be—that must be. Live beyond the pain of reality with the dream of a bright tomorrow. Use hope and imagination as weapons of survival and progress. Use love to motivate you and obligate you to serve the human family.
>
> We have the faith and God has the power to see us through. March on till victory is won. Thank you very much. Keep hope alive.

12

Globalization:
The Promise and the Peril

Jawaharlal Nehru Memorial Lecture
New Delhi, India
November 20, 2007

Let me express my thanks to the Jawaharlal Memorial Fund for their invitation to be a part of this great tradition in this great nation, India. Our presence today comes at a moment in time so pregnant with promise and peril.

I want to thank the minister of state for foreign affairs, the Honorable Anand Sharma, for sharing your vision of a plan to continue growing while lifting the rural poor from the shackles of poverty. The loss of human potential because of poverty and inattention is too great a burden for any nation to bear. I am encouraged by the huge role that Indian Americans are playing in America in global technological development and the more than eighty thousand Indian students in America investing more than $3 billion a year.

I am more than encouraged by your willingness to help institutionalize the Martin Luther King–Mahatma Gandhi lineage with some reciprocal scholarship plan between African Americans and Indian students with cultural exchanges. Such cross-fertilization makes all of us stronger, and heaven happy. You have been such generous hosts, allowing me in these few days some measure of travel and to drink deeply from the wellsprings of your spirituality and culture.

My journey to India has long been anticipated. I wanted to see the land of the world's greatest and largest democracy. The land liberated by the science of nonviolent resistance led by the great and prophetic Mahatma Gandhi with young Nehru at his side. They used love, suffering, sacrifice, and political acumen as weapons of hope and change. They shunned the zero-sum game of mutual destruction.

I have gone to see the Taj Mahal; I visited the temple Swaminarayan Akshardham. I could not resist going back twice with my family. It was so informing and enlightening; it both heightened and deepened our religious journey, giving me a renewed sense of the roots of the Christian religion. The influence of Indian spirituality on our faith must be greatly appreciated.

There were other sites on our itinerary. I wanted to see Gandhi's birthplace. Instead, I visited the place where he was assassinated, and I laid a wreath. I reflected on the kings of scientific nonviolence and how Gandhi and King were brutally killed. But death for neither was a period but merely a punctuation mark, a comma, a pause, as they transitioned into greater service in their next life. Graves could not contain them. They live fresh in the hearts of freedom lovers who struggle every day.

We remember Gandhi, Dr. King, Nehru, Jesus, and Mandela, but too often we do not adhere to their lessons of peaceful coexistence over threats of war and annihilation. These times test the courage of our leadership. Those who would be declared leaders must know the perilous road is never risk free.

The roots of great changes in South Africa and North America and the freedom movements around the world are all witnesses that much of that force emanated from India. The irony is that so many of these leaders were jailed or killed pursuing the noble proposition of freedom, yet their sacrifices fueled the liberation movements the world over. Gandhi's use of soul force to resist evil remains relevant. He saw violence as a weakness to resolve conflicts, not a strength. There is no future in violence.

The giant technological advances must not dwarf our moral

mission to defend the poor, deliver the needy, and set the captives free. We are not advancing if we lose our compassion or sense of human values that really matter. Reports from the World Bank indicate that the average percentage of the global poor is 21 percent, or 1.1 billion people, who live on less than a dollar a day. Africa has the largest share at 46 percent; South Asia, 32 percent; East Asia and the Pacific, 15 percent; Latin America and the Caribbean, 10 percent; Eastern Europe and Central Asia, 5 percent; and the Middle East and North Africa, 2 percent. Thus the 15 percent living in poverty in the United States is better than the global average, but still pitiful for the richest nation in the world.

As we celebrate major markers of human freedom and democracy—the end of the slave trade, slavery, and colonialism—one of the most devastating legacies was the denial of access to education and thus the benefits of development that come from education. Strong minds break strong chains. Let's dispel any myths that the gulfs between the surplus culture and the deficit culture are natural. They are "normal," but that "norm" can change.

In today's emerging and dynamic world, diverse and adequate education must be the norm. The gap today is not a talent gap; it's an opportunity gap and too often an investment gap. We must educate our youth in sufficient numbers to sustain hope and growth.

In this new and inclusive world, so connected by technology, there is a force called globalization. In this new world, half of all human beings are Asian, and half of them are Chinese. One-eighth are African, and one-fourth of them are Nigerian. One billion-plus are in India alone. In the Western Hemisphere, English is a minority language.

Two-thirds of North America's neighbors speak Spanish. When Mr. Putin and Mr. Bush meet, they represent one-eighth of the human race; it's a minority meeting. Most people in the world are yellow, brown, black, non-Christian, poor, female, young, and don't speak English.

It is this world that we are called on to serve, to help lead to higher ground. In this world, students must remain energetic freedom fighters, and they are called on to do at least three things: (1) study diligently and succeed; (2) don't look down on those who could not get the opportunity; and (3) lift others as you climb and bring others along.

After the labors of Nehru and Gandhi and Dr. King and Mandela, we are free from slavery and colonial rule for the most part. The goal of our struggle was never simply freedom; it was equality. Freedom is a prerequisite in the fight for equality. But even beyond equality it is not enough to be coequals on a sinking ship.

We must have a value system beyond equality. We must have a vision beyond decadent values of greed and war and conquest and power. We must heal the whole community. We must secure the environment. End unnecessary wars. Have a one-big-tent vision. One measure of who we are lies in how we treat the young in the dawn of life, how we treat the poor in the pit of life, and how we treat the old in the sunset of life. The genius of the biblical character Joseph, of Mandela, Dr. King, Jesus, Nehru, and Gandhi was that they were not limited merely by ethnic considerations. They had majority visions to lift up the lot of all the people.

I want to lift up some perils and promises of globalization. In this new technological world, a one-world economy bound by a scientific network of communications, I never seem to be astonished that you can fly from Chicago to New Delhi or Bombay nonstop. Or how we can fly from Chicago to London or Paris in just six hours. But our new capacity for speed must not outdistance our moral commitment to do right, to be just and practice compassionate.

Globalization.

We are inextricably bound. In this tightly connected puzzle, every piece matters. In this quilt, every patch matters. Nazism, fascism, anti-Semitism, racism, nuclear weapons—these cancerous poisons cannot be contained; they keep us on edge. They metastasize really fast, and they kill.

Globalization is full of promises and peril. Global energy can warm us and transport us or it can be used to manipulate prices to control and polarize us. It can also instigate a war in Iraq or sustain a genocidal war in Darfur.

Globalization.

We can share research on global diseases and do delicate surgery from a foreign land to a faraway place; or search for cheap labor and undermine human growth and opportunity and disrupt nations.

Globalization.

Global terror is a car bomb or a suicide bomber. It can also be undrinkable water, crippling poverty in the midst of plenty and protracted genocide. Global terror is sometimes the unmelodious voice and misguided voice of hate, but often it is the voice of the unheard, the dispossessed, and the desperate.

In my nation, the United States, globalization and technology have increased our capacity for violence at home and around the world. We are fighting a war in Iraq using weapons—semi-automatic weapons, Uzis, M-16s—weapons that are being made legal again in America. We've lost nearly four thousand Americans in Iraq in four years; each year we lose thirty thousand at home to gun violence and one hundred thousand more are injured.

Globalization.

Global banking. It can spread capital and resources and development to the far reaches downward thru microloans, or it can spread upward with reckless schemes of exploitation. For example, the subprime lending schemes in the United States have 2.2 million families in danger of losing their homes to foreclosure.[1] A 10 percent decline in housing prices will amount to $2.3 trillion in economic losses, according to Goldman Sachs. Economic damages to financial services companies could be as high as $400 billion. And these companies may be forced to cut lending by $2 trillion—which could trigger a major economic recession.

The rich got rich quick; the poor are victims of inflated markets, redlining, and corrupt pricing. Globalized banking without moral values is triggering a worldwide economic tsunami. The water came in at the bottom of the ship, but now those on the deck and at the captain's table are running for cover.

Globalization.

In the end there is a need for environmental security. I remember the accident at Chernobyl.[2] At first the journalists said the Russians have a problem. But then the wind blew, and Europe had a problem. Then the wind blew some more, and the cows in Washington State had a problem.

Any war can unravel world security and progress and destroy our global quilt.

I want to appeal to you today to go forward with hope and not backward by fear. Increasingly, in this dangerous tension between globalization as perils or promises, our heroes are often political fear manipulators, smart people who become corrupt, or generals who promise us security through a bomb or a gun.

The fact is, Gandhi was right; the British generals were wrong. Mandela was right; the South African military was wrong. Dr. King was right; the Southern governors were wrong. Jesus was right; Rome was wrong.

I appeal to you today from this pillar of democracy and great spiritual strength and character—let's take the world to another level. Somebody has to make sense in this world. Somebody has to go counterculture. Global technology and capital must not remain unaccountable. It must not dwarf our moral imperatives.

Dr. King would often say, "Vanity asked the question: Is it popular? Politics asked the question: Will it work and can I win? But morality asked the question: Is it right?"

It may not be popular or politic, but our moral compass must not be compromised. Use globalization to end poverty and illiteracy and to end the HIV/AIDS epidemic. Use globalization to provide drinkable water and end hunger and to overcome fear and polarization. Use our diplomatic strength. Get the Middle East peace talks back on track. Use our strength to end the futility of trying to isolate Iran and Syria.

In conclusion, after a century of struggle, we are freer but increasingly less equal and more threatened. We need global peace, global racial justice, global gender equality, global children's and labor rights, and global health care. We need a new global vision. This struggle between dark and light continues. How can we forget the tragic pain and paralyzing fear of the dark morning of 9/11; terrorists hit New York City and Washington and Pennsylvania, and innocence was destroyed.

Let's not forget 9/11/1906, when Gandhi emerged declaring *satyagraha* as the lasting, enduring truth and source of joy. No cowardly acts of violence can put out the light of Gandhi's insight and commitment to truth. If we just reference 2001, 9/11 has a dark side; but 9/11/1906 unleashed the light, transformed nations, and cannot be put out.

The continuing hope and light may not come from 10 Downing Street or the Kremlin or the White House. It may come from some stable in Jerusalem, some manger where some at-risk child is born. It may come from some remote village in India on the Ganges River. It may come from some Martin King in southern Alabama or from some Mandela on Robben Island. Or it may come from some John of Patmos or some Gandhi or Nehru or some Bhutto from South Asia.

We are not sure where it will come from. But God has worked in marvelous ways down through the years. Of those who sought to do his perfect will of serving the least of these, John of Patmos saw something we should embrace today. He saw "a new heaven and a new earth"; he saw the old one pass away; that God has promised to wipe away our tears and to bring beauty from the ashes. That God, in whatever name, empowers us—empowers those on the ground to get back up again because the ground is no place for a champion.

Let us break the modern shackles, the barriers that keep humanity from recognizing its full potential. We need not reinvent the wheel. We have the keys, the use of soul force. It is in the power of *satyagraha*—soul force. We can overcome our tendency to hold fast to racial and religious bigotry.

Let's try something different tonight. We've tried war. It's a time-tested failure. Let's try something different tonight. Peace. Let's wipe out the sin and not the sinner. We need each other. Let's heal the breach. Friend and foe are trapped in the same house. As fire rages, as terror bombs explode and anger abounds, we need water, not gas and bullets. We need hope, not fear; love, not indifference. We have survived apart, now let's do a greater and more difficult thing. Let's live together as brothers and sisters and not perish apart as fools.

13

Dedication of the Martin Luther King Jr. Bridge

Danville, Virginia
September 18, 2008

Today we name a bridge after the Reverend Dr. Martin Luther King Jr. Today we honor the man whose leadership tore down the wall that divided us and enabled us to build the bridge, the bridge to a new South, a new America, and new race relationships, where brothers and sisters, black and white, lions and lambs, can lie together and find peace in the valley.

We honor him because of the way he lived, the way he served and was martyred—murdered as a hated man at the tender age of thirty-nine. Ironically, he was a man of love and peace who was so hated and despised. He was vilified and killed at thirty-nine. But God controlled the long arm of history. Dr. King would say unearned suffering is redemptive, and truth crushed to earth would rise again.

We survived the crucifixion of June 1963, when white policemen used violence, billy clubs, and fire hoses to attack peaceful black civil rights protesters who simply wanted to remove the wall of segregation and cross the bridge of reconciliation. And today we celebrate the resurrection, a new hope, and the new joy. The wall had to come down.

As President Ronald Reagan said near the Berlin Wall on June

12, 1987, "Tear down this wall." He challenged Soviet Union leader Mikhail Gorbachev to dismantle the physical symbol dividing families in East and West Germany. When the wall was up, East Germans were shot trying to climb the wall. But when the wall came down, when the demolition forces of justice succeeded, reconciliation could begin. Dr. King led the demolition crew and faced a fierce headwind.

Today we celebrate a bridge of tailwind, looking forward to a bright future of reconciliation and shared relations and shared growth. But forty years later, we are freer yet less equal. We have the most poverty since 1960; there are more children in schools on food assistance without health care; there is rising unemployment; there are incentives to close plants and send jobs abroad rather than maintain plants and attract more.

We need to do less bombing abroad and build more bridges at home, more roads, more schools, more railways, and put America back to work. Bridges at home and fewer bombs abroad is the key to our future and global security. Dr. King served, suffered, and sacrificed his life. In the truest form of Jesus and Gandhi and Mandela, our debt to him continues to be compounded. Those who blocked school doors and unleashed dogs and misused police power lost. Dr. King and the nonviolent suffering servants prevailed.

Dr. King only wants in return that we love one another, that we heal the wounds, that we heal the breach, and that we keep building bridges over troubled water. As long as the wall of the cotton economy of slavery and segregation was up, the entire region was limited. Its growth was stunted. Behind the walls were ignorance, fear, hatred, violence, and negative economic growth.

But when the cotton curtain came down we could see and appreciate each other more fully as sons and daughters of God. When the wall came down, new industry could become possible in the new South.

When Dr. King dreamed in 1963, we were living in an emergency state of racial fear and friction. Blacks could not vote; we could not use public facilities and public parks and theaters. Our money was counterfeited; we could not rent a room at the Holiday Inn or buy ice cream at the Howard Johnson's.

But today hope abounds. We are a new and better nation. But it is not enough to be better; we must also be better off. We cannot merely share poverty and pain; we must share possibilities and growth. This bridge named for Dr. King must be a bridge to somewhere. The bridge must lead to reindustrialization, must lead away from divisive schemes that lead to Wall Street collapse, which has injured so many Americans and weakened our stature in the world. It must lead to reciprocal trade policies that will allow American workers to play on an even playing field.

The bridge must lead to the erection of more bridges, levees, and schools. The bridge must lead to lower tuition rates and more Pell Grants for our children. The bridge must be a place where jobs stop being exported and drugs and guns stop being imported. It must lead to more futures and fewer young funerals. It must embrace Dr. King's last dream, a poor people's campaign, where all could come together with a job, income, education, and health care.

A bridge that leads us from racial battleground to economic common ground. It leads us to healing. It must lead to this most profound profession in 2 Chronicles, chapter 7, verse 14: "If my people who are called by my name will humble themselves and pray and seek my face and turn from their wicked ways; then God will forgive our sins and heal our land."

Today, long live the promise of God. The sacrificial service of Dr. King and the hope will take all of us to a bright future.

14

Global Peace and
Unity Conference

**The Islam Channel
(satellite television)
October 22, 2008**

Let me express how honored I am and what a joy it is for me to be invited to address the Islam Global Peace and Unity Conference. I want to thank the Islam Channel for making this invitation possible.

A couple of weeks ago I had a physical bout that I am now overcoming successfully. It was premature to come to the United Kingdom at this time, but I look forward to coming soon. The idea of this conference is appealing to me. It is both a moral and a practical imperative. Global—peace—unity are all critical themes that must become reality and flesh.

Today science and technology seem to have outdistanced our moral imperative to do justice, love mercy, be humble and not arrogant and lifted up, feed the hungry, defend the poor, deliver the needy, and not allow pride to blind us from the possibilities of peace, development, and growth.

Amazingly, today we have the capacity to feed all of the world's hungry, and yet hunger abounds. We can clear up every polluted stream, and yet lack of drinkable water is the crisis for many of the world's poor. We are so close to peace and shared interests of survival, and yet there are those who insist that nuclear development is a form of security. In reality it makes us less secure.

Religions must lead the peace effort for coexistence and not coannihilation. It must lead us from ethnic and religious battleground to economic common ground and on to moral higher ground. The underlying assumption is that there is room for all of us under one big tent. We must remove the barriers of pride that limit our capacity to see each other fully and relate to each other faithfully across lines of religious dogma and ideology.

Today, we are often endangered by religion and by political fanaticism in the name of religion. We should be made secure by religion. Too often the toxic wars of religious chauvinism lead us to worship the surface and not the substance called for by the character of our religion. In the book of Micah the question was raised, "How do you worship? Do justice, love mercy, and walk humbly before thy God." Political zealots who abuse religion never hear this formula for worship.

We should be known by these acts of mercy and help, not by symbols of violence. We must focus our joint efforts beyond the boundaries of our religious dogma—find a cure for HIV/AIDS and cancer; drinkable water; denuclearize the world; close the huge gap between the fortunes of the North and the poverty of the South. To address world poverty, which leads to sickness, death, recycled fear, often terror and sometimes war.

Too often we succumb to marketing schemes; religion is seen as a commodity for some and not a blessing for all. But religion is a serious proposition in the quest to connect with God. And yet in my Christian religion, Jesus made a profound statement: hope has universal application. "Love the lord your God with all your heart, with all your soul, with all your mind and with all your strength" (Luke 10:27). But there is another line that completes this formula: "And love your neighbor as yourself." That part challenges our earthly human relationships one to the other. What does it matter if you love the Lord your God but will not feed the hungry or clothe the naked or care for the sick and then blow a trumpet for peace and reconciliation?

How do you love the Lord whom you have *not* seen and then

disavow your neighbor whom you *have* seen with acts of terror? It is a contradiction in terms. States must protect religious freedom and our celebrations. The extreme actions within any of our religions do not reflect the character of true religion. They are just characters in the religion that distort, deny, and misrepresent. In America, white Christians advocated slavery and often held lynching events after church on Sunday.

Those are acts of terrorist characters. But the character of the Christian religion is not terror. The German Christians in the name of God drove the Holocaust, made Jews as the anti-Christ. That was demented and perverse theology, with a twisted view of the world that cost the lives of millions. That was not the character of religion; that was some sick characters of coopted religion.

For those who see Islam as inherently violent, with an unquenchable thirst for violence, self-demolition and, thus, cannot be trusted—that's not the character of Islam. Christians who wear crosses, Jews who wear yarmulkes and the Star of David, Muslims who embrace their symbols—must find a common thread to make heaven happy and the earth rejoice.

Even with conferences like this the unresolved Middle East crisis is never far away from our consciousness. Israelis and Palestinians, Christians, Muslims, and Jews must accept each other and find a new formula for peace. Egypt, under President Anwar Sadat, found a way to increase trade, remove barriers, build bridges, and relieve fears. It required courage, even sacrifice to the point of death. But history has redeemed his risk. Sadat presented us with a healthy plan for adversaries to live together.

That model called for Israel's right to exist with security and protection from a hostile environment. It called for Palestinians coexisting with their own state, with an avowed commitment to coexist with Israel. It called for us to live and let live, give our children a chance, and open up a bright future.

The model is sound politically and morally. Sadat's view of mutual recognition and shared security remains the key to the future for the entire Middle East. We should seize this moment, this opportunity, to expand Middle East peace. Neither verbal nor ideological threats of nuclear development will lead to prosperity, growth, or peace.

It's time for us to take some bold actions of bridge building. We need to begin to dream of sharing, reconciliation, and peace, not a final military Armageddon. In the Old Testament the question was raised, "When will there be peace in the valley?" The answer was, when lions and lambs lie together (Isaiah 11:6).

That seems to be impractical. These are two extremes. Lions are strong, arrogant, and greedy, and they eat lambs for sport. Lambs are comparatively slow and meek and are no competition for the lions. But the biblical message is that the extremes must find common ground.

What do they have in common? Neither lion nor lamb wants the water poisoned. Neither lion nor lamb wants toxic rain on their backs. Neither lion nor lamb wants the forest to catch on fire. If the forest is on fire, the lion-ness and the lamb-ness are irrelevant. Both are cooked and destroyed. Surely if lions and lambs can find common ground, then we of Christianity, Judaism, and Islam must find that similar spot in our hearts and minds.

I look forward to meeting with you and engaging in a more meaningful dialogue in the coming days.

15

The Journey of
Our Ancestors

**Inauguration of the African
Renaissance Monument
Dakar, Senegal
April 3, 2010**

I wish Dr. King, whose assassination we observe on April 4, and Dr. W. E. B. Du Bois, George Padmore (Trinidad), President Leopold Senghor (Senegal), President Kwame Nkrumah (Ghana), and Patrice Lumumba (Republic of the Congo) could be here today to see their dream of the African diaspora family reconciled, to see Pan-Africanism flourish.[1]

Congratulations to the current Senegalese president, President Abdoulaye Wade, on such a powerful idea. The African Renaissance Monument is a powerful idea from a powerful mind, fertile with imagination and a sense of history. Strong minds break strong chains. Access to education remains the strongest weapon in our arsenal. You can't teach what you don't know. You can't lead where you don't go. Education matters.

This statue is dedicated to the journey of our ancestors, enslaved but not slaves. This is a singular great moment for me. Fifty years ago this year, Julian Bond and I were jailed for trying to use public facilities, in my case a library. The same year as your independence fifty years ago, we were revolting on both sides of the Atlantic. Today I am in Senegal as we seek to freeze our journey in this statue. Yet the statue is also art. And art lives. So it's a living memorial with unfinished work to be done.

Europe and the United States for too long had a plan for slavery, colonialism, and subjugation. We have a plan for dignity and freedom. Our renaissance is to wipe out war and malnutrition, provide drinkable water, wipe out HIV/AIDS, wipe out hate and hostility, and measure our character by how we treat the least of these, the poor and those on life's margins.

Now President Wade is giving us a new frame of reference. We must act now.

We must build links between African institutions, universities, museums, and recreation centers with those from the Caribbean, Latin America, and the United States, wherever the diaspora leads. We must send students and research professionals to these institutions and receive our students, professionals, and researchers; create rich lines of communication, have an exchange of experiences, and learn more than one language.

The renaissance today is history in poetry. This weekend we dedicate the statue, commemorate Dr. King's life legacy, celebrate Easter, and remember Haiti's earthquake victims. The renaissance is history and poetry. Look at the convergence of events this weekend. We recently experienced an earthquake in Haiti. That crisis gives us another chance at redemption, at how we have treated the beleaguered Haitian nation. Really, Haiti is the first country of all of those in the diaspora and the motherland that fought for and won a revolution from 1791 to 1804 against French colonialism and slavery. It was the shining light of freedom in the long dark night of slavery. Due to Napoleon Bonaparte's ongoing defeat by black Haitian slaves waging a successful independence war, Napoleon was weakened in his will and with loss of his troops. The United States bought more than half its territory from France in the famous 1803 Louisiana Purchase. As a result of black people's independence movement in Haiti, Napoleon was forced to sell to the United States present-day Arkansas, Missouri, Iowa, Oklahoma, Kansas, Nebraska, Minnesota, North Dakota, South

Dakota, parts of New Mexico and Texas, Montana, Wyoming, Colorado, and Louisiana.

At that moment Haiti was the only free African country in the whole world. In the 1800s Thomas Jefferson imposed a trade embargo on Haiti. Subsequently, because Haiti was the only freed African people throughout the globe, in the 1800s the United States and France embargoed Haiti and denied its growth. Toussaint Louverture, a former domestic slave and leader of the Haitian revolution, went to France to get his recognition papers, was kidnapped in France, and died in a French jail. Why must Haiti be remembered in a certain special way? They were the only shining light of hope and freedom in the whole African world. In the 1800s, sixty-five years before slavery ended in the United States, they were the biggest threat to slavery in the whole world. The idea of Haiti had to be crushed. And the crushing of the idea of Haiti continues to this day. The French and the United States demanded that Haitians pay reparation to the enslavers, a debt burden they carried in 1947. For the liberation struggle the French never forgave Haiti, the United States never thanked Haiti, and the Catholic Church remained much too silent. Eighty-five percent of Haitians are Catholic.

I think about Gorée Island and its Door of No Return. Off the coast of Dakar, the island of Senegal was the largest slave-trading center in Africa from the fifteenth to the nineteenth century. And we still weep at that door at the thought of our ancestors not returning as they moved onto European slave ships. But today let the word go forth that we have returned with strength and more power than ever. We've returned as teachers, philosophers, skilled tradesmen, mayors of cities, governors of states, members of Congress, and, indeed, the president of the United States.

What a journey from the hull of the ship at Gorée Island to captain of the ship of state of the most powerful nation on earth! Mean men sold us to be their slaves. Apparently God distributed us to save the human race. Wherever we are in the world, there's a struggle for human rights; there's a struggle for the poor; there abides the struggle in international law, human rights, self-determination and economic justice. Wherever we are, we make the case that we cannot just globalize capital. We must globalize human rights, workers' rights, women's rights, children's rights, health care and a healthy environment. The renaissance is alive.

This statue is a place where we might tell our children our story. They need to know. Tell them at the Door of No Return that they might know that we have returned. Tell them that the tragedy of Gorée Island ultimately did not prevail. Tell them a mighty Africa stands. Renaissance and reconciliation, declaring one Africa, one currency, the United States of Africa, declaring hope is alive and Africa is resurrected. Sin has abounded, but grace and hope have abounded even more.

16

Speaking Truth to Power

Christian Aid Conference
London, United Kingdom
October 21, 2010

I want to express my thanks to Christian Aid[1] and all of you antihunger activists for giving me the chance to join you here in London today.

Dr. King taught us to strive for the moral center. During slavery and colonialism the "left" said, "Be kind to your slaves." The "right" said, "They are property, be harsh if you need to." It was the abolitionists who said, "End slavery!"

The moral center rejected both wings. It was another bird altogether. The abolitionists fought to end slavery, not to reform it or defend it. They were not pursuing kindness or harshness but dignity—the moral center.

Often our great heroes are not heads of state or corporate executives but instead are freedom fighters who fought for the moral center: Dr. King, Gandhi, Elie Wiesel, Archbishop Tutu, Mother Teresa, Nelson Mandela, and Christian Aid leaders. They sought to pull down walls of division, walls of archaic power, and replace them with bridges of cooperation.

As we fight for environmental security and the right to breathe free and have drinkable water we must be good stewards of the earth. We are renters, not owners. We do not have the right to abuse the earth. The earth is the Lord's and the fullness thereof. We must nurture it. Air, land, water, seasonal changes—there is no limit to its abundance. When we abuse the earth it fights back with fierce winds, fires, cyclones, hurricanes, and quakes. We do not want to invoke the wrath of God.

When we try to decide how to act as Christians, and what we should fight for, we need to refer to our "mission statement."

Luke 4:18: "The spirit of the Lord is upon me, because he hath anointed me to preach the Gospel to the poor, he hath sent me to heal the brokenhearted, to preach deliverance to the captives, and recovering of sight to the blind, to set at liberty them that are bruised."

We are tasked to bring the good news to the poor. To feed the hungry, to clothe the naked, to shelter the stranger, to house the homeless, and to study war no more. We applaud Christian Aid, fighting for international aid for the poor and sensitivity in government. Aid to the poor makes heaven happy.

The Scriptures say it is a way of leading to the Lord. It's a way to secure hope, to build bridges, to create allies, and to end the trauma of darkness and fear. It is the best way to fight terrorism.

We applaud Christian Aid for trying to see the world through the eyes of Jesus. It's a way of looking at the world through a door, not a keyhole.

Jesus viewed the world bottom up; Herod viewed the world top down.

Jesus saw life from the manger up; Herod, from the mansion down.

Invariably in these austerity budgets, prosperity and preservation are protected top down while poverty and pain are exposed bottom up.

Down through the corridors of history our faith calls us to speak truth to power, which is risky. Moses cried out, "Pharaoh, let my people go!" (Exodus 9:1). He showed great courage. The people also had to have faith to let Pharaoh go and choose dignity and hope over shame and fear.

We find Jesus born in a slum, a minority, without citizenship in Rome.

We find him feeding the hungry fish and bread.

We find him converting fishermen into advocates for the poor and the hungry.

We find him declaring, in summation, that the most powerful weapon of hope and survival and faith is love. Loving God is a big part of the criteria for ascending into God's kingdom, but the whole test is even more difficult—to love your neighbor as yourself. By extension Jesus died and sacrificed for the unknowing, the uncaring, and the ungrateful.

He loved because it was the right and fulfilling thing to do. He made clear his mission was to bring good news to the poor.

Paul takes us into another dimension. It's not just how we deal with flesh and blood, people we can touch, but political priorities, how we handle powers and principalities, how we handle structural disorders, how we deal with wicked men in power.

Ephesians 6:12: "For we wrestle not against flesh and blood but against principalities, against power, against the ruler of the darkness of this world, against spiritual wickedness in high places."

It may be that good men and women end up carrying out their orders, the orders of wicked men. For example, military budgets are too high because we make unusable, exotic, and expensive weapons that don't work and are useless for the type of warfare today.

Isaiah warns us to study war no more, to beat swords into plowshares and spears into pruning hooks. He's asking us to stop studying how we kill and use our engineering skills to build peace, not military-industrial complexes. For example, taxes are too low on the very wealthy, combined with excessive offshore tax dodging. There is also the unregulated "bankster" policies that drive home foreclosures and wreck the economy.[2] There is also a pattern of disparities in our modern society—not just police profiling, but bank lending, home foreclosures, the prison-industrial complex, housing patterns, and so many other public-policy disparities. These policies produce benefits for the wealthy and hardships for the poor. Thus we protest! We march! We speak truth to power!

Dr. King marched across the segregated South to protest the lack of civil rights and the lack of dignity. Nelson Mandela endured twenty-seven years of jail to protest the lack of human rights and the lack of dignity.

Black Consciousness leader Stephen Biko gave us his martyrdom in the cause of justice.

Anglican Archbishop Trevor Huddleston marched to defend the poor and protest apartheid.

Jesus bore the cross even unto death.

So we will keep on marching, keep on speaking out for the poor and against policies that cut services for the poor, which will have the effect of increasing the numbers of the poor. We march for equal access to education, against home foreclosures and to end unnecessary wars. We march to water the roots not just the leaves.

When the elites talk about austerity they're usually talking about austerity for the poor, austerity for working families. This is ham-and-egg justice that is inherently unfair—it sounds good, but the chicken only gives up an egg, the pig gives up a leg. The wealthy sacrifice a little but the poor suffer a lot.

There is a lot of talk on the television about how the United States and the United Kingdom are suffering from an economic hangover and now we have to sober up and clean up after the party. The problem is the people who are being asked to do the cleanup are not the ones who had the party. The poor in the United States and the United Kingdom were not invited to the big global party of the last few years. Instead they were handed foreclosures and lost pensions and outsourced jobs and cut wages and now cuts in social services.

Today those of you who fight for the poor will speak truth to power about these budget cuts. The ones who had the big party should pay to clean it up. We will have to wrestle with politics, talking to elected officials, representing the poor inside the system and outside on the streets. As I said, the apostle Paul spoke in Ephesians 6:12 about powers and principalities: "For we wrestle not against flesh and blood but against principalities, against power, against the ruler of the darkness of this world, against spiritual wickedness in high places."

I know that Christian Aid applauds that the governmental budget maintains international aid. That's good. The problem is this austerity budget, these cuts in social services, will create more poor people in the United Kingdom. Five hundred thousand job cuts means 500,000 fewer house notes, 500,000 fewer cars bought, 500,000 fewer vacations, fewer park visits, and fewer Christmas gifts.

These cuts do not take on banking bonuses.

But they do cut the social safety net.

These cuts do not hit those who wrecked the economy.

They do not reform globalized trade.

They do not stop unnecessary wars.

But they do cut the social safety net.

These cuts won't help build affordable housing.

They won't get more poor and working families' children into Cambridge and Oxford.

They certainly won't close the inequality gap, but rather they will widen it.

The rich will not lose a house or a second house, will not miss a vacation, will not have to drop a child from private schools—but these cuts will push more middle- and working-class families into poverty. Where is the social safety net in an austerity budget? What drove the current economic crisis were the bankers, unfair trade policies, and unnecessary war.

The poor and the workers are now paying for an unnecessary war in Iraq that they opposed. The poor and working families are now paying for banker exploitation that they opposed. Their taxes are paying to clean up the mess now. And soon five hundred thousand more of them will be out of work. We will revive the economy by investing bottom up not by cutting services top down. We could grow our way out, but too many are choosing to cut our way deeper into a hole. We could revive by investing in building new schools, houses, clinics, roads, sewers, and bridges.

So, sisters and brothers, let us remind our leaders that the social safety net is important, that the cuts will afflict the poor and hurt working families, that an austerity budget is not the bottom-up investment in the future that we need.

In Matthew 25:31–40, Jesus taught us that we would be measured by how we treat "the least of these." Our character is measured by how we treat the hungry, the dispossessed, the disenfranchised, and the abandoned. So it makes me very proud to stand with Christian Aid today, a multicultural, multiracial organization that fights to end world hunger and fights against global warming. My brothers and sisters, thank you for standing up for the poor and dispossessed of the world. And thank you for inviting me here to London to share these past few days with you. Through all of these challenges don't you stop dreaming because it's difficult and circumstances are dire.

John, on the Isle of Patmos, dreamed of a new world, a new heaven and a new earth, while the old one passed away—a world where God would wipe away our tears.

Dream until we wipe out poverty.

Dream until we have clean water and breathe free.

Dream until we wipe out global hunger.

Dream until we study war no more.

Dream of a world of hope, love, and joy.

I love you all. Keep hope alive!

17

Dr. King in Today's America

2011
(occasion uncertain)

In this time of remembering Dr. Martin Luther King, we should remember him not as a celebrity but, as he called himself, as a drum major for justice. Dr. King had a dream, but he was much more than a dreamer. He helped transform America, yet he never held a public office nor amassed a great fortune. He was a bold leader, a committed organizer, and he wasn't tranquil. He forced America to look at hard truths and grim realities that most preferred not to face.

Many people wonder how Dr. King would feel today. The best measure is to look back to what he said and did. He surely would have been pleased at the progress that has been made, the end of legal apartheid. He would see the integrated football and basketball teams, and watch as people cheer the color of the team uniform not the color of the players' skin, and be cheered. The freedom agenda that he helped to marshal has made great progress.

At the same time Dr. King would surely tell us that the dream was still under attack. Amid islands of hope he would see oceans of despair. He would be amazed by March Madness of the college basketball playoffs, but troubled by graduation sadness after the same athletes dropped out of college. A leader deeply committed to nonviolence, he would be appalled by an America marked by the violence of the attempted assassination of Representative

Gabrielle Giffords[1] (one of one hundred thousand injured in gun violence every year) and the deaths of the innocents, Americans killing Americans (about thirty-two thousand killed each year). He would see the reaction—the sale of even more guns—as a sign of our moral incapacity.

Dr. King called for "a true revolution of values," understanding that the moral world would "look uneasily on the glaring contrast of poverty and wealth." And, sadly, he would see more people in poverty today than in his years and far more concentration of wealth among the few.

Dr. King realized that in wealthy America unemployment is both cruel and unnecessary. "There is nothing except shortsightedness to prevent us from guaranteeing an annual minimum and livable income for every American family." He argued not for welfare but for work: "We must develop a federal program of public works, retraining and jobs for all—so that none, white or black, will have cause to feel threatened." He would not be satisfied with a Congress that has failed to act while long-term unemployment hits record levels and over twenty million Americans are in need of full-time jobs.

Dr. King publicly opposed the war in Vietnam, understanding that the money for the war on poverty at home was being lost to the war in the jungles overseas. He would be pleased that Americans are overwhelmingly committed to defending Social Security, Medicare, and Medicaid. But he would be alarmed by the cuts now envisioned in programs vital to people, even as we squander an estimated $3 trillion on wars in Iraq and Afghanistan. "Congress," he reported, "appropriates military funds with alacrity and generosity. It appropriates poverty funds with miserliness and grudging reluctance. The government is emotionally committed to war. It is emotionally hostile to the needs of the poor." And so he would find it to this day.

Dr. King would recognize the progress that has been made, but he would not be dancing; he would be organizing. "Change," he taught, "does not roll in on the wheels of inevitability, but comes through continuous struggle." And he would indict us for our silence in the face of current conditions: "The greatest tragedy of this period of social transition," he argued, is "not the strident clamor of the bad people, but the appalling silence of the good people."

To honor his memory, let us end the silence!

18

Bold Leadership, New Direction

Doha, Qatar
May 9, 2011

We invest in war; we wish for peace. The United States spent $3 trillion on the Iraq War according to the latest estimates. It was collateral damage; we had the wrong information; we aimed at the wrong target and were disconnected from those who attacked us. It cost us lives, money, and honor with no one accountable.

Given the cost and futility of war, will we learn?

We speak of the Arab world. In reality, today the Arab community, European community, African community, Asian community, and the US community are all inextricably bound. We are one world. The US president Barack Obama and his staff on May 2, 2011, watched the death of Osama bin Laden in real time. Today we watch the battles in Libya and Syria in real time. Live deaths and battles appear to us from cameras and satellites globally. We are increasingly living in one world, no longer separated by oceans and mountains or languages.

We have survived apart, and distance has created many problems. We now have a greater challenge; we must learn to live together. It's a greater challenge than surviving apart but infinitely more rewarding. There is a tension today as we see the ugliness of war and speak of peace. Coexistence and peace are dismissed as unrealistic and "soft." So we don't pursue them vigorously. We speak of justice; but we reject one set of rules that inherently demands a redistribution of resources and opportunity.

The prophet Isaiah admonished we should "study war no more and beat our swords into plowshares" (Isaiah 2:4). We are called to turn weapons of destruction into tools of development; develop peace scientists and not war scientists. We focus on who uses the weapons and who can purchase them. We use our best scientists and technology to pursue war, not to invest in peace. We take a special pride in sending a man to the moon but not the same joy and research for wiping out malnutrition, malaria, and HIV/AIDS and responding to disasters.

The trauma of September 11, 2001, is now behind us. America was hit, and thousands of innocent people were killed. The drama of May 2, 2011, when bin Laden was killed, is now behind us. Both of these traumatic events are now in our rearview mirror. The question is: Can we go another way? Or must we prepare for round two and recycle the violence? We must choose reconstruction over revenge and retaliation. We must choose active dialogue and development.

We espouse democracy with theory and rhetoric. But we choose control and domination over growth. The United States evolved with slavery and an imperfect democracy coexisting; with an imperfect democracy and suppressing the rights of women coexisting; with an imperfect democracy and denying minorities a role coexisting. When African Americans rose up and brought freedom in America it was not due to communism or foreign intervention or interference. It was born of our own quest for dignity.

Astonishingly, in early 2011, with the antigovernment protests of the Arab Spring, you don't see the flags of foreign countries being burned. We see the tension of the vast body of educated people who are unemployed; the uneducated who want to become educated. We see corrupt and repressive governments. The desire for change is legitimate and bottom up.

What changed in the Arab Spring? In the fullness of time, people's minds changed. The insult level changed. The quest for dignity changed. And the outlet to tell our story changed.

Mental transformation is irreversible. The Arab world will never be the same again. Every country will feel this change at its foundation.

The fresh winds of democracy are blowing across the Arab countries. It is irreversible. It can't be contained; don't fear it. Embrace it. The wider the base, the deeper the foundation of people with opportunity, the stronger the government. I repeat, large numbers of educated but unemployed people, with corrupt and repressive leadership that sees the world through a keyhole and not through a door, will not work.

It never works. We must choose one big tent where all are in and none are left out.

We define democracy as of, by, and for the people, bottom up, versus all for the few, top down. But we embrace concentrated power and privilege where too few people have too much and too many have too little or nothing. Peace and a vast body of unemployed and uneducated youth are irreconcilable with democratic dreams.

Along with classmates, I was arrested in 1960 in Greenville, South Carolina, trying to use a public library. At that time the great divide was race and apartheid in South Carolina and South Africa, and European and American colonial conquest in the Third World. Today the great divide is between the surplus culture at the top and the suffering culture at the bottom—with the middle class shrinking. We're outsourcing labor to cheap markets and then insourcing content from those same cheap markets. The shrinking middle class is creating tension and oftentimes scapegoating.

At the end of the road of wars are tombstones, not pots of gold and cooling waters.

The extremes of poverty, desperation, and oppressive governments make for easy recruits to terrorism and self-immolation fighting wealth and power. High walls and weapons stockpiles cannot stop the will to kill and be killed in the quest for dignity.

Peoples' backs are against the wall, and they are revolting—extremes begetting extremes.

Where are we finding universal peace and order or a globalization that works? We glimpse the future in global sports competition. On the athletic field (whether the Olympics in Atlanta or Athens, China, London, or Qatar), whenever the playing field is even, the rules are public, the goals are clear and referees transparent and fair, people work hard and live with the outcomes. The winners have a sense of joy; the losers lost the game but keep their dignity; so they are all winners.

But when you globalize capital with the total advantage to the investor and don't globalize human rights, workers' rights, children's rights, human rights, or environmental security in a world connected by social media it will no longer work.

Our foreign policy in a global world should not be foreign to the best of democratic values. The democratic doctrine must include international law, human rights, self-determination, economic justice, transparency, and leadership with sensitivity.

Today in the North–South gap of nations, too much is spent on the military, building walls and not enough investment to build bridges. We have an addiction and fantasy of violence as a vehicle for change. Generals wear stripes and bars. But ultimately leaders who sacrifice create benefits that have longer life spans. It is Gandhi helping India overcome Britain's colonization. In the United States, segregation brought forth Dr. King. It is Mandela leading the struggle against apartheid in South Africa, using suffering as his weapon.

It is the Egyptian uprising in the Arab Spring, using massive nonviolence and noncooperation with oppression to create one of the most phenomenal revolutions of our time. It tells us that there is an alternative to violence, that nonviolence works. Too often we think peace is naïve and war is a remedy, and thus some choose conquest over coexistence. But the key to peace is a fairer distribution of resources rather than weapons.

Lastly, there is no substitute for leadership that has strength, character, courage, and is transparent. President Barack Obama has these basic characteristics and is facing a tremendous head wind of resistance. When I look at him, one sees a man with a good mind, the courage of his convictions, a work ethic, and an inclusive vision that's broad and bold, along with a healthy sense of religion that allows for ecumenicity and operational unity.

President Obama has these characteristics, but he is being attacked at every level domestically. His trust and religion are under attack; his birthplace is under attack, his academic credentials, his motives and ideology. But like an eagle he keeps soaring without a need to come down.

We have our problems: more and more billionaires; three hundred yesterday, but today we have over one thousand. That is extreme concentration of wealth.

We bailed out the banks without mandating lending and reinvestment. The foreclosed homes are exploding. We gave the richest tax cuts. We're involved in three wars.

President Obama has a high moral compass, but he needs help to tackle these foreign and domestic challenges.

The progressive changes in the Arab Spring will become the Arab Summer and the Arab Fall and the Arab Winter—until spring comes again, when the bright morning of universal justice appears for all. One day, we will have shared economic security. Shared justice. Shared education. Shared opportunity. A means to make a living, and universal health care for our children.

On that day, lions and lambs lie together; the powerful and the meek commune together; and none shall be afraid. I know what changed in the Arab Spring. There needs to be a refusal to submit to corruption and an undying yearning for democracy—and the will to fight for it. Deep within our souls we all share this yearning for democracy. On all continents, in all languages and cultures, we share this yearning for freedom and dignity. So we must go forward by hope and not backward by fear.

19

Racism and Conflict

**The UN International Day
for the Elimination of
Racial Discrimination
March 21, 2012**

It is a distinct honor to speak to you today on this anniversary of the UN Declaration on the Elimination of Racial Discrimination. The March 21, 1960, massacre of blacks protesting their identity cards in Sharpsville, South Africa, triggered this annual commemoration. We must not betray the victims of this terrible disease of racism by growing weary in our struggle to end this degenerative, emotional, immoral disorder called racism.

Racism is the great moral flaw of our civilization; it is a state of sin. We've inherited it. It's been passed down through generations. Racism is driven by greed, the hound of hell, and accompanied by violence that is used to perpetrate this crime against humanity. Despite the ongoing struggle to end it, it remains, unfortunately, prevalent among us today.

This is not to deny progress. A few days ago I saw a film on President Lyndon B. Johnson in 1964 speaking to the US Congress making the appeal that America would be free from segregation laws, and ultimately he spoke of the right for all citizens to vote. It was an almost all-white and male Congress. It looked like a seventeenth-century textile convention. It was less than fifty years ago when President Johnson made that appeal. But in our lifetime we've seen that American Congress and that political culture change. Today people of African, Asian, and Latin descent serve at every level of both parties. There is even a woman speaker of the house in the US Congress.

We've now had African Americans and women secretaries of state: Colin Powell, Condoleezza Rice, and now Hilary Clinton. Now we have an African American president, Barack Obama, of American and Kenyan descent. We've seen fruits of continuous struggle. Walls are coming down and bridges are being erected out of the rubble of those walls. President Obama's victory was a redemptive moment for the United States and the world, overcoming so many years of legal and cultural separation, indifference and pain.

We must honor the United Nations and particularly the September 2001 Durban (South African) "Declaration against Racism." At the time, some major nations did not participate. Others walked out; others did not even endorse the final declaration, uneasy about addressing an apology for slavery, a call for reparations, and Palestinian/Middle East tensions. The Durban Declaration was reviewed in 2009, and now ten years later it is time to reassess it again and plan how to strengthen global infrastructures to eliminate racial discrimination.

Let's lift up some lessons learned for this discussion. The July 18, 1950, UNESCO (United Nations Educational, Scientific, and Cultural Organization) study made the case that blacks were *not* inferior, dealing a blow to Nazism and many prevailing pseudo-scientific race-superiority theories of that era. The fire of such virulent racist theories has not been totally extinguished. We must remain vigilant. While seemingly absurd today, race-superiority theories were widely accepted by scientists, legislatures, and religions throughout the world. But that study, like the Durban Conference, has had great impact.

Racism is immoral. It's a sin. It assumes that God made superior and inferior people. It suggests that God supports racism, which is untheological and untrue. Skin idolatry is ungodly. Racism is unscientific. It suggests that there are superior and inferior people based on genetics. There are many royal blood and racial blood theories to perpetuate power, inheritance, and lineage. I can assure you that if you were in a wreck and injured and needed a blood transfusion there is only A, B, and O blood types—royal blood is in short supply in blood banks.

These power theories based on race give the privilege to the powerful, advantaged by birth, no matter what they can or cannot do; others are disadvantaged regardless of their merit. Merit, character, and work don't have a chance in "race blood" theories.

Because it is immoral and unscientific and a threat to humanity, racial discrimination must be made illegal, as a deterrent to stop racist behavior.

In the United States we had to pass enforceable laws to prevent racial discrimination, to impede racist behavior. But the goal remains elusive.

Racism limits growth—it is exclusionary. It limits talent and stifles potential. You look at the great soccer teams, and you choose uniform color over skin color, direction over complexion, and region over race. That is the formula for victory and community. We can only say that we did not know how good football could be until everybody could play on the same team.

The great lesson that we must learn from soccer or football or track, with winners often coming from the most obscure places and among the poorest people—it may be a Kenyan runner, a Brazilian soccer player, a Jamaican sprinter, a gymnast from Asia, or a basketball player from the United States—is to keep everything above board with a plain purpose. What we learn is that whenever the playing field is even, the rules are public, the goals are clear, the referee is fair, and the score transparent, there is fairness. We can accept the outcome with grace and dignity. The inherent justice of these rules allows us all to be a winner. Whether winning or losing the game or event, no one ever loses his or her dignity. That is the key to the joy of the games. But racism creates an *uneven* playing field. It is exploitative. It is a form of violence that triggers a violent reaction. It gives emotional false security; it chooses inheritance over work; skin color over the human race; petty interest over the global community.

Racism is politically destabilizing and distorts the human personality. It is akin to gender bias and gender supremacy theories. When societies build laws and institutional structures on theories of race supremacy that's called a racist society. Inherent in such a society are the seeds sown for its eventual destruction from the inside out. These houses of racial exploitation are built on quicksand. They cannot withstand the winds of justice.

Jesus dealt with race theories when he declared that we are of one blood. He embraced the Golden Rule: a 1:1 ratio of "Do unto others as you would have them do unto you." Jesus gave us the moral high ground to challenge tyranny and tyrants. Jesus said you measure people by how they treat the least of these. It is your capacity to care and the choice you make (not your skin color, the choice you did not make) that measure who you are.

In the parable of the Good Samaritan, the question is asked, Who is my neighbor? Jesus gave this imagery: He said a man was beaten and left to die. In his stricken state he looked up and saw a man of his own religion, of his own ethnicity; he felt sure that help was on the way. That man of his own religion crossed the street and kept walking. Amazing indifference.

Another man of his own ethnic persuasion—the Levite—saw him lying there. He, too, crossed the street. But the Samaritan, a man of a different race, different complexion, who spoke a different language, from another country, who worshiped God differently, and didn't even have a green card, stopped and helped him up. He sought for him medical relief. Jesus then asked the question, Which of these was the man's neighbor? Obviously the one who cares, the one who comes to rescue in time of need.

If anyone's house is on fire, if the wind blows, we are all in jeopardy—whether it is a tsunami in Japan or an earthquake in Haiti.

In today's world there are no more foreigners. In this one-world house in which all of us live, where speed dwarfs distance and time, and with the click of a mouse we see one another around the world in real time, if any one room is on fire and the wind blows, we all are in jeopardy. So the security of each of us is based on what happens in the next room.

How do you fight this disease of racism? The winners are invariably long-distance runners who are willing to serve and sacrifice. Mahatma Gandhi said we must fight it by noncooperation with evil, with *satyagraha*—soul force. There is a moral imperative to cooperate with the good; likewise, there is a moral imperative to resist evil and oppression—thus boycotts, sit-ins, strikes, public demonstrations, and coalitions are all necessary to fight such a formidable foe.

Indifference can be an act of racism. Laws that protect race superiority must be abolished. Reject within you the spirit of false security based on race and embrace people beyond your comfort zone. That's why Gandhi adopted an untouchable. That's why Jesus glorified a Samaritan and in his last night on earth stayed with Simon the Leper.

Even though President Obama ushered in a redemptive moment for America and the world, the lingering cultural fears and theories and structures of inequality and racial fears remain. There are those willing to sink the ship just to destroy the captain. They are relentless in their attempt to marginalize him, using not-so-veiled code words. A congressman says from the well of the House floor, "He is a liar." Other prominent Americans argue, "He is not born here, he is not legitimate." Another says, "He does not share our religion; he is not a Christian; he is a Muslim." But through it all President Obama's nonreaction of reciprocating these acts is evidence of his strength.

Dr. King fought this moral flaw of racism that undermines justice. He realized that the race walls, racism, and expensive race wars that stand between the people and drinkable water and health care must come down. The walls between the people and medical treatment; the walls between the people and access to education; the walls between the people and the fair distribution of resources must come down. Our world remains much too entrapped in the spirit of violence.

Too much concentrated wealth; too much poverty. Too few have too much at the expense of too many who have not enough. There are too many countries rich by endowment but poor by exploitation. Rich soil and poor people should not go hand in hand.

Dr. King emphasized the immorality of racism. We should not have to be indifferent to the war in Liberia, where thousands were killed; nor to the war in the Congo, where six million were killed, nor to genocide in Rwanda. These intragroup wars of superior/inferior groups share the same burden of toxic racism.

Dr. King sought to lift us up to the lofty plane of justice and above the behavior that leads to unnecessary wars. Ultimately, racism (beyond being immoral and unscientific) must be vanquished. We must enforce laws that alter behavior and ultimately nurture attitudes that will lead to new relationships. Racism and racial discrimination are impractical. They make all of us losers. We never know what special genius you lose when racism blurs your vision of a neighbor's potential.

Dr. King was born in a Southern ghetto under segregation. Mandela was born in a village in South African under occupation. Gandhi labored under British colonialism. Jesus was born a Jew in the lineage of the prophets. He was born poor and an ethnic minority. He faced race discrimination under the occupation of the Roman Empire. He was born in a stable without protection from the elements. He was born under a death warrant with the edict of official genocide waving over his head. He was born the poorest of the poor at the very bottom of Jewish society. His special genius would have been lost if those who engaged in acts of genocide under Herod's command had been successful in killing him as a baby (Matthew 2:1–13). He was a peasant from Galilee. He escaped to Egypt as an immigrant/refugee, and yet from that lowest of places he emerged as a source of salvation and healing. He turned scars into stars. He became a light of hope committed to defending the poor, delivering the needy, and setting the captives free. He rejected corruption in the political and religious order. He rejected class and racial exploitation.

Remember as the world changes, yesterday's colonized people living in colonial disgrace are still faced with today's degradation of immigrants. Their children become your new neighbors, citizens, and elected officials. Not rampant racism but a moral message. Let's try something different. We've tried racism, war, and degradation, and the pursuit of justice without mercy. Let's try something too often untried. Let's try *love.* Let's try sharing. Let's try caring. Let's try one set of rules. Let's try hope. Let's try beating our swords into plowshares, our spears into pruning hooks, and study war no more. We tried war and racism; they're failing. Let's give love and peace a chance. Not simply as poetry but as a lifestyle and government practice.

The author of 2 Chronicles puts it well when he says, If my people who are called by my name, not by their race, who are called by my name, not by their class, will humble themselves and pray and seek my face, and turn from their wicked ways, God will forgive their sins and heal the land.

As we commemorate this occasion and seek the world of our dreams, let's keep healing.

Keep hope alive.

20

Reflections on
Fifty Years of Struggle

**Lincoln Memorial,
Washington, DC
April 24, 2013**

What a blessing it was to have been here fifty years ago as one of the host of witnesses, excited and fresh from jail in Greensboro, North Carolina. To hear the collective voices of Walter Reuther from labor, the booming voice of A. Philip Randolph (Brotherhood of Sleeping Car Porters), Floyd McKissick (Congress of Racial Equality), Whitney Young (National Urban League), Roy Wilkins (National Association for the Advancement of Colored People), John Lewis (Student Non-Violent Coordinating Committee), Mahalia Jackson (the Queen of Gospel), Dr. Martin Luther King Jr. (Southern Christian Leadership Conference), Bayard Rustin (chief organizer of the 1963 March on Washington) and to stand with Dorothy Height (National Council of Negro Women), Walter Fauntroy (Washington, DC, coordinator of the March on Washington), Jackie Robinson (the first African American to play in Major League Baseball), Ossie Davis and Ruby Dee (famous performers and supporters of progressive causes), Dr. Benjamin E. Mays (pioneering civil rights leader, author, mentor, and scholar), and so many others.

I had been to jail twice, once in South Carolina and once in North Carolina. Thank God for allowing me to be a part of an increasingly small group of witnesses who have been long-distance runners. We changed the South and the nation. Across these years we've connected Mason and Dixon, the line dividing the northern and southern United States. We couldn't have had the National Football League teams, Carolina Panthers in Charlotte, North Carolina, and the Atlanta Falcons in Georgia, behind the cotton curtain. We couldn't have had Louisiana State University in Baton Rouge (Louisiana) and the University of Alabama in Tuscaloosa (Alabama) in the college championship football game; or the Olympics in Atlanta, Georgia; nor could we have had the auto industry—Toyota, Hyundai, and BMW—in the South. But in the 1960s the civil rights movement broke down racial segregation in the South. It freed African American people from the superior–inferior structure of white over black. It did more than that. It broke the dam of social backwardness. Today, coming through are the flowing waters of industrialization, entertainment, and finance. Southern desegregation moved the entire nation to higher ground. Southern governors tried to block those New South opportunities. Our movement tore down walls and built bridges. Ironically, many who tore down the walls lay beneath the rubble while those who resisted now benefit from the new bridges. And yet we'd do it all again. It's by grace, not by gratitude and false praise, that we go forward with hope and not backward with fear.

It was important to support the living dream that was addressing the challenges of its day. The dream of 1963 was not the dream of 1968. In 1963 we addressed the barbarism of that day. From Texas to Florida up to Maryland we couldn't use a single toilet. We couldn't swim in the city swimming pool or skate at the skating rink. We couldn't buy ice cream at Howard Johnson's or rent a room at the Holiday Inn. There was not a black juror in the South. Only registered voters can serve as jurors. Washington, DC, was under military lockdown, with an appointed mayor. The dream of that day was to address the segregation, barbarism, and racial animus.

The dream in 1964 was for a Public Accommodations Act;

make barbarism illegal. The powerful words expressed by Dr. King reflected the historical longings of those who for too long had been locked out. Black soldiers at home had to sit behind Nazi prisoners on US trains during World War II. The American flag flew gently above them in the breeze, as they tasted the bitter fruit of institutional racism. They were sent to Europe to fight fascism, but on the same train with fascist prisoners black soldiers had to sit in the segregated section of the train. Under the rules of racism, even white Nazis had privileges over black soldiers. The dream lifted us from the stench of the blood of Medgar Evers (leader of the Mississippi NAACP assassinated in 1963) and the smell of Southern jail cells. They sentenced us to penitentiaries in Louisiana; they burned the buses of freedom riders in Anniston, Alabama; in 1963 they bombed four little girls in a Birmingham church; the same year they conducted a terrorist attack on President John F. Kennedy. It was this blood and these martyrs that gave urgency and content to the dream of 1964—the need for a Public Accommodations Law.

After the 1964 challenge of the Mississippi Freedom Party led by Fannie Lou Hamer in Atlantic City at the Democratic National Convention; the killing of civil rights activists James Chaney, Michael Schwerner, and Andrew Goodman during Freedom Summer in Mississippi; the Bloody Sunday of March 7, 1965, in Selma, Alabama, triggered by the death of Jimmy Lee Jackson; the beating death of Rev. James Reeb; the state police trampling of John Lewis, Rev. Hosea Williams, and Mrs. Amelia Boynton (on Bloody Sunday in Selma); the shooting of Ms. Viola Liuzzo after the march from Selma to Montgomery—the dream of 1965 became a Voting Rights Law.

The dream of 1966 was open and fair housing in Chicago. We were met with violent resistance. This was Dr. King's first sustained drive in the North. We focused on a stronghold of racism—the whites-only area of Cicero, Illinois. Dr. King said that in the Northern fight for decent housing he faced some of the worst acts of white supremacy. Up North turned out to be like down South. The dream of 1968—the Poor Peoples' Campaign—believed that there should be a foundation of education, health care, affordable housing, and a job below which no American should fall. With great reluctance Dr. King challenged the Democratic Party, the White House, and the Congress he had helped to elect. He argued that we should not shift our policy of a war on poverty at home to a war abroad in Vietnam. He felt that such a course of finding more security in bombs abroad than bread at home would lead to spiritual death. Bombs dropped abroad would explode in America's cities. This act of courage put him in isolation from the mainstream, but he said, "I will speak and I will be heard."

I was blessed to be with him, to watch him and listen to him in the moment of ecstasy in 1963 and in the morning of agony in 1968. He felt the air was leaving the balloon of his dream. He felt that our propensity for the arrogance of war was undermining our moral authority in the world. After having met for several days, I was with him in Atlanta, Georgia, when he agonized in our last Southern Christian Leadership Conference staff meeting with Dr. Ralph Abernathy, Andy Young, and his wife, Mrs. King. He said, "We're building a Resurrection City of tents, shanties, and shacks in Washington in front of the Lincoln Memorial where we once spoke of a dream. But today I feel like I'm fighting a nightmare." He said, "For nearly a week I've wrestled with a migraine headache. I thought maybe this is all I can do in thirteen years. Maybe I should leave now and head up Morehouse College and write books and travel. Maybe I should stop." Andy said, "Please don't talk that way." He said, "Don't say peace, peace, when there is no peace. Let me talk."

Then he said, "But I can't quit. I can't turn back. Sojourner Truth, Harriet Tubman, Frederick Douglass never quit, and they would not accept me if I quit. There is disunity in our leadership, going in different directions. While our leadership is different we are still friends. Maybe if I fast to the point of death they will come to my bedside and we could reconcile."

And then he broke out of his depression and said, "We're going to turn a minus into a plus. We're going on to Washington.

We're going to stop by Memphis. We're going back to the Lincoln Memorial. Maybe we'll engage in an act of civil disobedience, disrupt traffic in Washington. We must engage in radical sacrifice. It may be the end of us. We must end poverty, racism, militarism, and unbridled capitalism."

His three moods were very much like Jesus's three moods:

Let this cup pass from me.
As he prayed his disciples slept.
Not my will but thine will be done.

In the last fifty years we've seen mountains high and valleys low. We've seen the right to vote and its fruits. We've occupied offices that we used to not be able to get an appointment in. We're now congressmen, mayors, and state officials. We've had our high moments: the freedom of Nelson Mandela and the election of President Barack Obama—the crown jewel of our political effort.

And yet today all of our vast wealth military misadventurism continues; our subsidy of the wealthy continues; the attack on public education continues; the attack on public transportation continues; attacks on the public post office continue; attacks on small business continue; the largest jail industrial complex in the world continues and is expanding; private prisons with $1.5 billion per year in profits continue; pretrial detention up to five years continues; prison labor is expanding; Corrections Corporation of America is on the stock market; just locking up Americans for sport and profit continues. There's too much hate, too much violence, too many drugs, too many guns in the land. Our dreams are under attack.

Our challenge today may be to create discomfort in houses of power around the nation. We will use love and nonviolence with an appeal for mercy and understanding. There are too many poor people in a nation so wealthy. Today we are free but not equal. We have closed the separation gap between races but we've expanded the disparity gap between those who live in surplus and those who live in poverty. Free but not equal.

The unfinished business will require both courage and risk. It will require sacrifice. We must dream above the clouds of doubt and fear and cynicism. We still can dream of the constitutional right to vote and an end to the manipulation of voting in Virginia, North Carolina, Florida, and around to Texas. We still can dream of a new Civil Rights Commission, the conscience of our nation's government, coming back to life again. We still can dream of picking up the baton of the 1968 Poor Peoples' Campaign and reviving the War on Poverty.

Today, beyond inspiration, we must have a voting rights amendment and appropriations to wipe out poverty and not the poor. The fifty million in poverty and the near poor are unsustainable. Their dreams are being squashed. Their hopes dashed. Public housing closed and private housing foreclosed. Facing race profiles and stop-and-frisk laws in New York and stand-your-ground laws and bullets in Florida. There are thirty-one cities where black male joblessness is above 40 percent and six cities where it's above 50 percent.

The march in 1963 was not merely a cultural celebration. It was on the cutting edge of change and the challenges of that day. Its slogan was Jobs and Freedom. Thus, all of the great marches had a clear political agenda confronting the powers that be and the power that wants to be—to seek relief from misery, anxiety, and fear. This season of activity must be no less. All that we fought for is under attack again. We won bloody battles on the fields between 1861 and 1865 during the Civil War, but the US Supreme Court took them away with the stroke of a pen in 1896—the *Plessy v. Ferguson* decision legalizing racial segregation. During this fifty-year season we've won bloody battles, but with the stroke of a pen today's Supreme Court intends to take it all back. But we won't go back. We must have a political agenda that is designed to change the legal parameters and discourse of our nation. So it was then. So it must be now. Too many people have been pushed outside the tent of protection. We must end the proliferation of war. We need expansion at home over violence and fear. Revive the War on Poverty with appropriations and allow Dr. King to rejoice in heaven on his special day.

An assassin's bullet killed the dreamer. We must not kill the legacy of the dreamer and the prophet with mere celebrations and reflections. We too must remain on the cutting edge of today's challenges. While we may pause to look in the rear-view mirror, our purpose is to look out of the windshield. This search for our progress and "a more perfect Union" is real.

We have unfinished business. We want those who are inspired by him to follow him, not just admire him. To admire him is to quote his poetry. To follow Dr. King is to pick up the baton that was blown out of his hand. To follow him is to see the federal budget as a moral document. When the Congress is reconvened and the State of the Union is proclaimed, clearly in this season of too much violence, if we can have the constitutional right to carry guns surely we can have the constitutional right to vote—the very foundation of our democracy.

To follow him is to fulfill his mission. So keep dreaming—student loan debt forgiveness. Keep dreaming—restore public housing and end private housing schemes while bailing out banks. Clearly, if we can bail out Wall Street banks and the auto industry we cannot leave Detroit, Birmingham, and Selma bankrupt and blowing in the wind.

Keep dreaming. Use that vote and use those marching feet. When President Obama takes the economy from four million jobs down to above the plus zone, stand with him and march for more. And when the president tries to provide health care for all Americans, stand with him. When he bails out our industrial base and gives them a chance to recover, stand with him. When he ends the war in Iraq, stand with him.

Keep dreaming. End the stop-and-frisk policy and racial profiling because racial profiling is unconstitutional. We should go to higher ground. Instead of stop-and-frisk" start stop-and-employ. Ask him, "Hey, brother, do you have a job?" Stop and provide health care, stop and provide Head Start, stop and build high-speed rail and the cars to go on them; stop and regain trust between the police and the people. Stop and love somebody.

We've tried loveless justice. It's too brittle. We've tried just love. It's too sentimental. Dr. King studied Paul Tillich's 1954 book *Love, Power and Justice,* and he was right. We need all three—love, power, and justice. But most of all we are not our brother's and sister's "keepers." We are our brothers' and sisters' brothers and sisters. And we want to do unto them, as we would have them do unto us. Those who obtain mercy must be merciful. It's not merely the color we seek to change, but direction and character. It is a new vision that we seek. John said it best on the Isle of Patmos in the pit; he saw a new heaven and a new earth (Revelation 21–22). The old one passed away, and he promised to wipe away our tears.

But above all stand with a conscience. Vanity will ask the question, "Is it possible?" Politics will ask the question, "Can we win?" But conscience asks the question, "Is it right?" If the principle is right," it may never be popular or politic, but it will prevail. Stand through it all because there's hope. Stand on those dreams. You've come too far to turn back now. Say to the White House and the Congress, "Partner with us." Let's make Dr. King happy again. Make him happy by permanently protecting our right to vote with a Voting Rights Amendment added to the Constitution. Give him the joy of reviving the War on Poverty. Make him happy. Give him the joy of ending more and more high-tech wars, of ending the reduction of budgets for schools and trauma units. Make him happy.

I know it gets dark sometimes. But this land is our land. We the people (with the help of God)—Jew and Gentile, Muslim and Christian, male and female, gay and straight, black, white, red, yellow, and brown—can heal this land. I know it's dark sometimes, but the morning cometh. Keep dreaming. Keep healing.

"If my people who are called by my name will humble themselves and pray and seek my face and turn from their wicked ways . . . I will forgive their sins . . . and heal their land."

Keep hope alive.

21

Tribute to Nelson Mandela

United Nations
New York City
July 18, 2013

Today we honor Madiba (Nelson Mandela), the honorable servant leader, a fighter in the streets, a fighter in the courts, a fighter in prison, and a fighter in the hospital.[1] He has never stopped fighting. Today we offer prayers for his continued recovery. Fifty years ago, during the great global revolt against racism in America and South Africa, Martin Luther King Jr. and Mandela were jailed. Fifty years later, they're both exalted. They are the great moral authorities of our time.

A lot can be said about his twenty-seven years in jail. Some stayed longer. It is not the length of time in jail but the choices he made. He chose reconciliation over revenge. He chose coexistence over coannihilation. He chose healing of deep wounds over perpetuating hurt and scars. He chose hope for the future over hostility for the past. He chose to redeem, forgive, and move on to higher ground. He chose equal rights for all rather than reciprocal pain. He sought to end tyranny not just to change its color. It is tyranny that is the sin against God.

Every now and then there emerges among us a human being of such rare and vintage quality that the light of their unusual witness affects the state of our collective humanity. The sound of the genuine is not a common occurrence these days, but I submit to you that in the presence of an original sound the deep dissonance of our world is made palatable, if not transformed into something harmonious and symphonic.

And it is also the case that in the presence of such a towering figure not only must the world stop and take notice, but also perhaps more importantly, we are inspired to find a more excellent way. It is with this in mind that I join with you in celebrating the life and witness of Mr. Nelson Mandela. Nelson Mandela is, as he has always been, a man of unusual grace, tolerance, and courage.

For who else could have single-handedly transfixed the social imagination of an entire nation, while he himself languished in the darkness of a narrow South African prison? And even now, as Mr. Mandela enters into what might well be the evening of his years with the sun soon setting just beyond the reach of his loftiest achievements, he is again summoning the attention of the world as he beckons us to be mindful of the fragility of life. For let us never forget that it is because of the life and personal sacrifice of Mr. Mandela that South Africa is a different nation today.

The dark night of apartheid and racial disparity did not come to an end on its own. For those of us who have dedicated our lives to the possibility of freedom and equality understand with amazing clarity that social transformation was an intentional act. The South Africa we celebrate today is the result of the deliberate struggle of millions of people both on the continent and around the world who somehow believed that midnight could not last forever. And so we fought.

Sometimes we fought with tears in ours eyes, but we kept on fighting. We lost a few friends along the way, but we kept on fighting. And there were times when we had to take up our struggle against the better judgment of the so-called civilized world. But James Russell Lowell was right in December 1845 when he wrote his poem "The Present Crisis":

> Truth forever on the scaffold, Wrong forever on the
> throne,—

Yet that scaffold sways the future, and, behind the dim
   unknown,
Standeth God within the shadow, keeping watch above his
   own.

Mr. Mandela's twenty-seven years in prison are a reminder to all of us that sometimes you have to be willing to toil in a tight place to create open space for democracy to flourish and grow. We here must highly resolve that Nelson Mandela did not henceforth labor in vain. And even now, as we celebrate the event of his birth, we must do more than give mere commendation to his struggle. That kind of empty commemoration is too small for Mr. Mandela. For if we are to truly celebrate the man in whose name we have dared to gather, then the aim of this celebration must be as big as he continues to be.

And how do you celebrate a man called to fight for truth in a world built upon many lies? The answer is simple: by taking our place among that great cloud of witnesses so that we, like them, might push our shoulders against the great wheel of history until one world dies and another world is born.

For let us never forget that before he was a President Nelson Mandela he was a freedom fighter Mandela. And today we cherish his struggle and take our peace from the solemn pride that must be his to have laid such a costly sacrifice on the altars of freedom and love. Today we honor the courage of Mr. Mandela, as he is for us a constant reminder that truth crushed down to earth will invariably rise again. Mr. Mandela is our living response to all the cynics who seek to convince us that the world will forever be as it is now.

In closing let me simply say that that world will little note nor long remember what we say here today. But it will never forget the living witness of Nelson Mandela because we all are standing on the shoulders of Madiba. We are a little taller sharing his vision. We see a little farther. Because of his sacrifice we work with a little more diligence. We're made better because of him. And he stands among the towering figures of the human spirit: Dr. King, Gandhi, and Fannie Lou Hamer.

We don't know how long he will be able to labor among us. But Shakespeare said it best in *Romeo and Juliet*:

> When he shall die,
> Take him and cut him out in little stars,
> And he will make the face of heaven so fine
> That all the world will be in love with night
> And pay no worship to the garish sun.

22

We Seek a New Heaven and a New Earth

Fiftieth Anniversary of the March on Washington Washington, DC August 24, 2013

Dr. Martin Luther King Jr. was a democratic—small "d"—evolutionary revolutionary. He didn't just *speak* truth to power. He *confronted* power with truth and with nonviolent direct action around morally just causes. Dr. King was born during ugly white occupation and segregation—American apartheid. He confronted a legally segregated Jim Crow Southern society and won a 1964 Civil Rights Act. He confronted discrimination in voting based on race and won a 1965 Voting Rights Act. He confronted segregated housing in Chicago based on law and custom, and in death he won a 1968 Open Housing Act. He confronted a Democratic president (whom he had supported) over a violent war in Vietnam that undercut a peaceful war on poverty in America, and helped to bring that immoral war to an end.

Dr. King wasn't assassinated for dreaming. He was assassinated for acting and confronting. We must not destroy Dr. King's legacy with sanctimonious celebrations, commercialism, and sweet stuff. And when he was killed he was broken hearted. The dream had turned into a nightmare as he looked into the rural and urban zones of America where fear and neglect reigned throughout the land. He saw an economic system and exploitative trade policies that were taking jobs out of America. He saw too much war abroad. And he saw neglect of the poor at home.

His assassin didn't kill a dreamer. He killed a militant marcher. And we must not kill the martyr by leaving him in Atlanta, the site of his birth; or remembering him in DC, the site of his political and economic analysis, and his beautifully articulated dream. He was killed in Memphis, marching with and fighting for garbage workers. Dr. King would have celebrated the joy of our progress: the freedom of Nelson Mandela, the end of apartheid, and the presence of democracy in South Africa. He would have rejoiced at the election of Barack Obama. He would have seen these as crown jewels. But he also would have seen the unnecessary war of choice in Iraq, the pain of economic stagnation and high unemployment, the retrogression of a conservative Supreme Court, and the racism of a dysfunctional Congress.

He would have seen fifty million Americans in poverty and another fifty million on the borderline of poverty. He would have said, "There's too much poverty and hate and war and violence in America and in the world in 2013." Dr. King saw the federal budget as a moral document containing the nation's priorities. Today we are still the richest nation on earth, but we have no peace dividend. We project ourselves as winners, but we're losing the middle class to unemployment and poverty. Our trade policy is failing; our war policy is failing; Wall Street was bailed out and is winning; but Main Street was not bailed out, and it is failing.

I'm asked all the time what's the difference between Dr. King and other political leaders? What's the difference between moral leadership and political leadership? I'll tell you what the difference was and is. As a moral leader Dr. King could articulate a vision, describe his dream, inspire us, and motivate us to action—and he did. But he couldn't write and pass laws, and he didn't have the power of the purse.

But political leaders then and now do. The president and the Congress have legislative and appropriation power. And I—like

Dr. King—refuse to believe that the bank of justice is bankrupt. I refuse to believe that we are willing to spend about $3 trillion on the two wars in Iraq and Afghanistan and their aftermath but then our political leaders tell us we don't have any money for jobs, job training, education, health care, housing, a clean and sustainable environment, or for rebuilding America and our infrastructure. I don't believe them!! I think their moral compass and their priorities are off.

I saw Dr. King in his moments of joy in Washington, DC, on August 28, 1963, proclaiming his "I Have a Dream" speech. I saw him in agony in Atlanta deliberating over the future of the civil rights movement. I saw him in mental anguish and assassinated in Memphis. But I know that the dream of 1963 was not the dream of 1968. He had a dream in DC in 1963, but five years later in Memphis many of his former allies became adversaries. You know we love martyrs, not marchers. Many today suffer historical amnesia. They admire only the 1963 "I Have a Dream" King. But they forget the militant marching, pro–garbage workers and non-violent revolutionary Poor Peoples' Campaign King.

His last plan for DC was the Poor People's Campaign. There he had planned to give a speech at the Lincoln Memorial overlooking Resurrection City, made up of tents and shelters filled with all the poor of America represented. He had planned to demand a shift from a war abroad to a Poor People's Campaign at home. Dr. King said his mission was to disturb the comfortable and comfort the disturbed.

You may be uncomfortable here today—the site where Dr. King was planning the Poor People's Campaign and creating a national priority to resurrect the poor from poverty.

Instead, today we have the absence of a vibrant Civil Rights Commission, the conscience of our government; we have stand-your-ground laws in Florida; voter disenfranchisement in North Carolina, Texas, Ohio, Wisconsin, and elsewhere; stop-and-frisk laws in New York; unjust marijuana laws; a trade imbalance that's sacrificing jobs; guns and drugs in, jobs out; home foreclosures;

a flag of surrender on the war on poverty; congressional leaders pedaling fear and hate upon this president; high-tech wars; tax cuts for the rich, budget cuts for everyone else; hospitals and trauma units closing; public housing closing; shrinking public transportation and stopping fast rail; banks bailed out, but student borrowers and homeowners locked out.

Dr. King would have said, "Too much war and too few jobs, too little social uplift and too much moral bankruptcy." He was killed with his poll numbers going down but his values and standards were going up. He said, in essence, reject me if you will—those who once embraced me and marched with me—but I will speak and I will be heard.

This is a political march. It is not a commemoration or celebration. When he was alive, he was fighting in the era of barbarism, before the 1964 Civil Rights Act and before the 1965 Voting Rights Act. There was no premature celebration.

Today, our forward movement is being confronted by a backlash movement on the right to vote, a backlash on affirmative action, a backlash on public education, a backlash on public transportation, a backlash on publicly assisted housing, and a backlash on public health care (the Affordable Care Act). But our character is still being measured by how we treat the least of these.

In the end, Dr. King came to believe that the triple evils of *racism*, *unbridled capitalism*, and *reckless militarism* would destroy our nation. We are determined that those three blind mice—the nightmare of racism, unbridled capitalism and reckless militarism—will not lead us down the rat hole of destruction.

Today, we have come here to march and to protest and to make a witness that we still believe the arc of the universe is long but that it bends toward justice. We are here today to affirm that faith, hope, and love will guide our path along the road to freedom, jobs, and justice.

God help us fulfill the dream of Dr. King.

23

Free, but Not Equal: Keep Dreaming

**Third World Summit
of Mayors, Officials, Africans
and African Descendants
Cartagena, Colombia
September 18, 2013**

I want to thank the mayors and legislators from the United States and around the African diaspora for their steadfast work in convening this family of African descendants and their generous invitation for me to be with you today. It's a great honor and privilege to be with you here in Colombia. Colombia is a robust and beautiful country of forty-five million people, full of natural resources and talent—mining, agriculture, oil, and fishing. Colombia is our neighbor to the south, part of our global neighborhood. We are all neighbors, and in today's social media world there are no more foreigners. Colombia stands in a unique position poised to become a leading trading partner with the world. The mayors who have convened us are linked by the common lineage of the slave experience and the struggle for abolition. I commend the theme and goals of this summit to connect and network people of African descent from all over the globe to share best practices and develop a common agenda for the future. I share with you the abolition of slavery dates of several of our countries, beginning with Haiti.

- 1805: Haiti is the first country to declare independence and abolish slavery. Haiti fought gallantly against the French and became a beacon for all the Caribbean seeking decolonization.
- 1824: Panama
- 1829: Mexico
- 1851: Colombia and Ecuador. But it wasn't until 1993 that Colombia passed Law 70 giving recognition and rights to Afro-Colombians.
- 1854: Venezuela and Peru
- 1888: Brazil

We in the United States don't fully appreciate that there are more Africans in South, Central and Latin America than in the United States. The slave trade started through this region; the United States was the caboose. We did not end slavery in the United States until 1865 following a brutal civil war.

- 1957 to 2000: Africa. African independence stretched from Kwame Nkrumah in Ghana (1957) to Nelson Mandela in South Africa, the last African country to overthrow structural oppression.

When I was a little younger and tried to read the Bible, I looked at the genealogical lineage of "begat, begat, begat" in Matthew chapter 1. It had no meaning to me. I was trying to get to some sentences and some parables. When they would say Jesus comes down forty-two generations after David, I had no appreciation of the power of forty-two generations of unbroken family continuity. The Torah, the Holy Book, and faith hold us together. The families in those sacred Scriptures may have gone through turbulence and famine and war or oppression, but forty-two generations of family continuity is powerful.

Most of us find it difficult to go back four generations; the power of our African diaspora families was broken through slavery intentionally. So for our Jewish brothers and sisters everything starts with a political event of the exodus and God delivering them from slavery across the Red Sea through the wilderness to Canaan, the land of promise. We are linked in that same journey from slavery to exodus to wilderness in search of our Promised Land of Canaan and beyond the mountaintop. Even though we fight for fair and just immigration policy around the world as people escape oppression, it's not like the slave experience where people were bought, sold, and exploited for profit for several centuries. The global system of slavery—a violent racialized form of immigration—for the African diaspora was the crushing of lineage and identity.

Our children must know about the linkage of slavery.

There is a scripture where the children of Israel got across the Jordan River. They got across because God intervened and not because of their own ingenuity. They were told to get from each tribe a rock as remembrance so that they would know how they got across the river. In time to come the children would ask, What are these stones? Tell them that they might know.

If they do not know they will honor false gods and make the real God angry. No one wants the wrath of God visited upon him or her. If you know the lineage of slavery then you will know how every one of these countries got here. You will know the reason for their present circumstances; you will know the future prospects for each of these nations. From Brazil to the Caribbean and throughout South, Central, and North America, African people in the lineage of slavery are still fighting to overcome oppression and marginalization. So we know by experience. We are known by experience. We each have a survival legacy.

Our very presence today is a miracle gathering. The fact that mayors can convene us, the government accepts us as gracious hosts, and we can meet with leaders of state—it's different. In the early part of the twentieth century, Trinidadian lawyer Henry Sylvester Williams (organizer of the 1900 Pan African Congress, London), Dr. W. E. B. Du Bois (organizer of the 1919 Pan African Congress, Paris), and others tried to have Pan African congresses. At that time, the very coming together of our people was seen as subversive and dangerous. I cannot emphasize enough the roots of the slave experience. Our Jewish allies will not let you forget the exodus, and Yom Kippur, and the role of Moses and David and why they need a state that is secure to protect them. It's rooted in five thousand years of history. We must learn from them. We must tell our story to our children and our children's children. We must sear the moral authority of our narrative into the very global conscience of all people and for all generations.

Dr. King would say the evils of racism, poverty, violence, and hatred stunt our growth and development. It hurts the oppressed and the oppressor. It limits the vision of the racists and the dreams of the victims. Racism is unscientific—it assumes that one group is inherently superior and worthy; the other group is inherently inferior and unworthy. The cultures are taught race supremacy in schools, churches, homes, and in the media. It is a very-well-taught lesson, too well learned by too many, and it must be unlearned.

Tragically, many victims of oppression learn the same lesson, internalize the lessons of the oppressors and lose the will to fight back. It is the burden of leaders to teach people they are somebody and fight back. We go through stages in this journey to the promised land of equality and justice. In the United States, for example, after 246 years of slavery, a civil war took place in which the union was saved and slavery ended. But the promises of abolition weren't kept. While we focus so much on Dr. King's "I Have a Dream" speech we forget the powerful words of the beginning where he opens by talking about the broken promises. "You promised shared dignity. You promised sharing the vote. You promised sharing public accommodations. You promised equal opportunity."

Stage one was to end legal slavery. Stage two was to end legal racial apartheid laws and segregation laws. Stage three the right to vote. But ultimately stage four must be addressed: access to capital, industry, and technology—economic justice. The social gaps are closed, such as barbaric, uncivilized laws of separation. But the economic disparities and inequalities in education and health care, jobs and employment, business contracts remain.

In other words, we are free but not equal. Many of our freedom allies are not our equality allies.

On the athletic field when I see Colombia or the United States in football, soccer, track, and basketball games we are very well represented. That's because the playing field is even, the rules are public, the goals are clear, the referees are fair, and the score is transparent. Broaden the tent; bring everybody in.

What is our mission? To even the playing field! Unfortunately, there are those who think that black inclusion is a zero-sum game—blacks come in and whites are removed. The fact is, inclusion leads to growth. When there is growth, everybody wins. Inclusion leads to expansion, not to elimination. Our leadership must have the moral authority to salvage the whole of the country, not just a part of it, "our group." Broaden the tent, and bring everybody in.

In the book of Genesis the biblical Joseph had an economic plan; he was an oppressed minority and endured slavery and false incarceration. His blueprint was to save the whole of Egypt. Dr. King in the voting-rights drive aimed to win and expand voting rights for all American citizens. The 1965 Voting Rights Act was not just for blacks, but women got the right to serve on juries; eighteen-year-olds got the right to vote in 1971 with a new constitutional amendment; students got the right to vote on their campuses; we won bilingual voting in 1975. Choosing the war on poverty and not the war in Vietnam was good for everybody. Broaden the tent, and let everybody in.

Mandela chose the soul of all of South Africa. He did not just replace white oppression with black oppression. His was an inclusive vision that was good for everybody. The biblical Joseph, Dr. King, and Mandela all had one thing in common: they were born on the margin, but they had majority dreams and visions. Ethnicity did not define the scope of their dreams. For inclusion of Afro-Colombians, a conservative remedy is what we call affirmative action for women and people of color. But there must be some plan beyond freedom.

In Europe it was a monster plan, the Marshall Plan—targeted investment with long-term, low-interest loans to rebuild Europe after World War II. It is unreasonable for those who have been locked out and left behind for centuries to simply join in. Perhaps we need a Colombian Truth and Reconciliation Commission, just as they had in South Africa to hear the stories of the victims and set an environment for education, economic development, and healing.

Perhaps you need a Civil Rights Commission just as we have in the United States to generate an annual report on the status of Afro-Colombians and to make recommendations for the full inclusion of Afro-Columbians in the social, economic, and political life of the country. The regions that we of the African diaspora now inhabit—Africa, South, Central, and North America—are endowed with riches and resources beyond measure.

We are neighbors linked by God. Through biology and history we are neither foreigners nor aliens. We are family. We may speak different languages, but we have the same message: human rights and democracy, not just the right to vote but to have access to food, education, health, housing, and jobs. We must end the flow of pain and hurt and replace it with hope and healing. All these societies that engaged in slavery and discrimination mirror one another. We are all made in God's image. We are all full human beings. We are all born with the unalienable right to participate. Broaden the tent; bring everybody in.

We must make big choices. We need to become peacemakers, not just peacekeepers. The status quo is too imbalanced. We must make peace. When there is no justice, there is and can be no peace. Whenever slavery has appeared, the same struggle for abolition has emerged.

We go from slavery to oppression to suppression to marginalization—where skin privilege and skin burden rule the day. The absence of slavery is not the presence of economic justice or political empowerment. The crisis facing Afro-Colombians mirrors that of the North American experience. While we have changed the visible landscape, financial resources are being withdrawn from mayors and cities; the president is under daily attack. In the United States we are still number one in infant mortality, number one in short life expectancy, number one in unemployment, number one in targeted home foreclosures, number one in denial of access to capital, number one in populating the jail industrial complex, number one in lack of access to health care, and number one in unequal education.

The United States is 5 percent of the world's population, with 2.2 million citizens in prison, of whom 55 percent are black. Afro-Colombians face a similar situation here. We have learned through conversations with many people on this visit—and through our own research—that Afro-Colombians are the most displaced people in the country. Displaced from land. Displaced from jobs. Displaced from an equal place in society. Displaced from high-quality education.

In the United States we call it gentrification. Oftentimes it's called eminent domain. Once it's determined that where we live is valuable and resourceful, then the government, under the pretext that our property is needed for public spaces, takes it away from us. Afro-Colombians were born and live in regions with some of the most resources—mining, fishing, agriculture, and tourism. But Afro-Colombians are not fully included in the economic life, industry, and future.

Look at advertising, flight attendants and pilots, government workers, private sector managers, universities, the banks and financial institutions. They do not look like Colombia. Afro-Colombians are underrepresented, still left behind in the margins. Look at government. Colombia is now the third largest country in the region behind the United States and Brazil. Yet Afro-Colombians are left behind and left in the margins. They need greater representation. Inclusion will be the key to growth, expansion, and development.

Afro-Colombians are between 20 and 25 percent of the total population, yet there are only nine members of Congress who self-identify as Afro-Colombians; three members of the Senate out of 102 (near 2 percent); and seven members of the House of Representatives out of 166 (near 4 percent). Of seventeen high-level positions at the Colombian attorney general's office, including eleven prosecutors before the Supreme Court, none are Afro-

Colombian. Out of sixty generals of the police and armed forces none are Afro-Colombian.

There must be Afro-Colombians in the cabinet and in the highest echelons of government. Political representation is key for Afro-Colombian inclusion. I say to my Afro-Colombian brothers and sisters, you must not have a deficit of will, spirit, or determination. You must aspire to run for political office at the local, state, and national levels. Be inspired and aspire. You have the power to change the nation. Afro-Colombians must be inspired to run an Afro-Colombian for president; reach for the highest office in the land. Arouse the sleeping giant, and dream *big* for a new Colombia.

Your running makes you a winner. If you do not run you have no chance of winning. Dream big, Colombia and people of African descent throughout the diaspora. We are slaves no longer. Across the diaspora we've won our freedom but still do not have economic parity or fair political representation. Equality means fair share, and government must see that inclusion, not exclusion, is the key. And Colombia needs peace and stability to fully unleash the economic potential of the nation.

We must wipe out race superiority and skin-color idolatry. We must affirm gender and race equality. None should be in the margins. We must end the marginalization of Afro-Colombians. We must do big things together. The good news is that we can overcome. I refuse to believe there is a deficit in the creative genius of social media like Twitter, Facebook, and the internet. I refuse to believe that we cannot tweet love, tweet care, and tweet education for all. Tweet justice. Tweet dreaming.

Dr. King was a dreamer. We can all dream above our pain and about our new possibilities. From the Isle of Patmos John dreamed of a new heaven and a new earth where the old one would pass away. No lonely island or condition can withhold the power of dreams. Dream hope. Dream healing. Dream of a successful peace process and of nonviolent conflict resolution. Dream of a day where drugs and violence no longer mar the image of a great Colombia.

And don't forget to dream of *one* Colombia. Dream of the day when lion and lamb lie together. Lions and lambs are two extremes. It seems they can never reconcile. What is it lions and lambs have in common? No matter how ferocious the lion is and how meek is the lamb neither wants acid rain on their backs; they don't want to drink poison water; they want to breathe free.

Dream of an environment free from pollution!

Dream of the day when we can wipe out malnutrition!

Dream of the day when we have clean affordable, drinkable water for our children!

Dream of an Afro-Colombian candidate for president—reach for the skies!

Dream of the day when we have health care facilities to care for the sick!

Dream when everybody has a house with indoor toilets and a running bathwater!

Dream, the blessed in the diaspora, of coming home on an annual basis and sharing your resources!

Dream of the day when we have free education to inspire and train our youth!

Dream of more trade and global markets! Dream of the day when the African diaspora is united, connected, and moving together to achieve common goals!

I know dreaming may be difficult sometimes. I know it's dark, but the morning cometh. I know it's difficult, but the Lord is our light and our salvation. Whom shall we fear? It gets dangerous sometimes. Though we walk through the shadows and the valleys of death we shall fear no evil. The Lord is with us.

Long live Colombia!

The formula is clear: if you want healing, do justice, love mercy, and walk humbly before thy God. And if my people, who are called by my name, and humble themselves and pray, and seek my face, and turn from their wicked ways, I will hear their prayer, forgive their sins, and heal their land. One Colombia.

Keep hope alive.

24

Launching a New University

Edwin Clark University
of Technology
Abuja, Nigeria
October 23, 2013

Introduction: Chief Edwin Clark is one of Nigeria's foremost educational and political leaders. With decades of service under his belt Chief Clark is launching a new technology-focused university in his home state in Nigeria. In doing so he will build an enduring and sustained legacy following the motto "strong minds break strong chains." At this dedication ceremony held in Abuja, Nigeria, to launch the university, Rev. Jackson was invited to keynote the event.

We are gathered here today in the great nation of Nigeria driven by one man's dream, one man's life work that accepted the burden of trying to lift a nation by its ultimate wealth and strength—the minds of its people.

Strong minds break strong chains.

With a population of 173.6 million, Nigeria is the home of the most Africans in the world. It is the home to the most talented people: thirty-six thousand Nigerian doctors in America alone, along with countless engineers, lawyers, and entrepreneurs. Nigeria is the source of so much of the world's energy, from oil and water, to solar and wind, to a vastly untapped agriculture. These underutilized and untapped resources, when used wisely, can lift up the nation and its people to higher heights. Nigeria is a nation of an awesomely endowed people.

One-eighth of the human race is African, and one-fourth of them are Nigerian. Nigeria in many ways is the center of the African universe with so much meaning for the continent and the rest of the world. I've been blessed to be a witness to Nigeria's evolution as a strategic partner to Africa's liberation over the past fifty years. Nigeria has always been central to the struggle of the Frontline States for liberation. The Frontline States—Angola, Botswana, Mozambique, Tanzania, Zambia, and Zimbabwe—were those original African countries that African liberation movements relied on in their struggle against European colonialism.

I first visited here in 1971 for the Africa-African American Dialogue with my wife, Jackie, and family, Congressman Carl Stokes, Percy Sutton, Attorney General Ramsey Clark, Bayard Rustin, and Whitney Young, who died suddenly on this trip.

In 1986, upon meeting Nigerian ambassador Joseph Garba in New York, we conceived an initiative to strengthen Nigeria's relationship with the Frontline States. Nigeria provided the plane for our delegation, and under the guidance of Nigerian external affairs minister Professor Akinyeme, we visited the Frontline States, the African National Congress leadership in Zambia, President Julius Nyerere at his home in Tanzania, President Kenneth Kaunda in Zambia, President Robert Mugabe in Zimbabwe, and Oliver Tambo, ANC leader in exile in Zambia. Throughout this very fruitful trip we were building solidarity and links between the African continent and African Americans. This was part of the process of solidifying Nigeria's commitment to the fight against apartheid and colonialism.

Today one of Nigeria's native sons, Edwin Clark, sprinkles sunrays of new possibilities for the future with the establishment of this institution in his name.

Dr. Clark is a visionary. He sees around the corner with the eyes of faith and the insight of vision. He possesses an unusually sharp mind and a heart whose love is boundless. He finds joy in watching others grow. He gratifies in sowing seeds that will bring forth crops and fruits in the unknown future. Because he perceives the future there will be fruits of education and fruits of technology. The key to the future of Nigeria and the world lies in science, technology, engineering, and math—STEM research and development.

Few live long enough, well enough, and reflect on their life's scorecard enough to be found worthy of an excellent grade and project into the future their will and testament to the people.

This school epitomizes Edwin Clark's life's testimony, his dream, his values, his patriotism, and his gratitude to God.

He knows the power of a developed mind and the waste of an unnurtured one. He sees the power of science and technology. The world has been made smaller and richer as science, with its speed, dwarfs distance with its technological advances. With modern technology we have the power to end poverty, as we know it, to provide drinkable water and nutritious food, to assure access to medicine and health care for all, and to wipe out the misery of poverty, ignorance, and disease. Science and technology make all of us neighbors. There are no more foreigners. We are all neighbors inextricably bound with a shared destiny and shared security.

Nonstop flights to Nigeria leave from the United States, from the United Kingdom, and from Moscow.

We now have computers on our wrists that connect the world in real time. This will be the university of the future—the University of STEM.

This university will create a legacy of service and sharing and future thinking. How much more powerful it is to leave a legacy of education for generations unborn rather than simply accumulating wealth and things for wealth's sake. Literacy is the key to liberation. Keeping people illiterate is the oppressor's weapon of control.

We often say the key to progress is unity. The Bible suggests the key is vision. Without vision the people perish (Proverbs 29:18). In a city where there is abounding blindness the one-eyed person is king. Visionaries have a seeing power to lift nations. This Edwin Clark University of Technology—and the presence of its living founder—establishes the power of vision.

How does one want to be remembered when you reflect in the afternoon of life?

For some it is to be like Alexander the Conqueror. For others it is to be among the elite and richest. For some it is to be a master of servants who are made to be servile. For others it is to be a general of great armies.

But with Dr. Edwin Clark it is simply to be an educator, humble in spirit, feeding nutrition for the mind. Jesus taught in one of his parables about the grace of being a seed sower (Matthew 13:1–9). The seed sower cannot control the outcome of the seed. He just knows the value of sowing and sharing rather than accumulating and hoarding.

Some seeds hit the rock. They will not germinate. Some will blow away in the wind. But others germinate. They give birth to fruit and possibility. Dr. Clark is a seed sower.

He is planting a future for this nation and this continent. He feeds and seeds the minds of the coming generations.

There is a biblical story where the children of Israel got across the River Jordan. They had survived the miracle of the Red Sea crossing, and now they met the turbulent River Jordan. They couldn't swim across. They had no engineering capacity to hold back the waters. They had no technological knowledge to build a tunnel. But God intervened and held back the waters. They got across without mud on their shoes, and they celebrated.

But then they were told to go and bring from each tribe a big rock and put each rock in the bed of the river. One might ask, "What value will the rocks represent in the triumph of Israel?" It is because you who saw the miracle, who saw the intervention of God, are celebrating what you witnessed. These rocks are a memorial so that in time there will come those who were not here who are beneficiaries of the miracle and they will ask: What of these stones? Tell them that they might know the mighty works of God. If you do not tell them they will not know and will ascribe their blessings to the false gods and reasons other than the truth. Both this ignorance and this arrogance will make the real God angry. Tell them Chief Clark loved them before they knew to love themselves.

Tell them this institution was made not by the hands of man but by the grace of God. Tell them when it's dark to hold on until the morning comes. Tell them to keep dreaming beyond their circumstances. Tell them to dream beyond their predicament. Tell them that when we are on the brink of war we still must choose peace. Tell them that we must choose negotiations with our minds over confrontation with our weapons. Tell them there is more power in humility than in arrogance and pride. Tell them to embrace love over indifference and hate. Tell them there is too much hate and fear and war in the world that we must reduce. Tell them that we must overcome the extremes of the surplus for too few and the suffering for too many. Tell them to remain morally centered.

So in order that we may please God, let this Edwin Clark University of Technology be a monument; let it be a miracle. Let us remember its origin, its purpose, and its mission. Let them know its founder. He chose those for the future he did not know so they would inherit such a righteous vision. Jesus, the master teacher, says if you give the best of your service for the least and in the interests of all Jesus will say to you in the last days, "Well done, good and faithful servant" (Matthew 25:23). So today we dedicate this school, and we thank a visionary.

In our anthems we say rather routinely, God bless Nigeria. With our good works we can do more than ask our God to bless us yet again. We can bless God by how we treat the least of these, how we lift up the downtrodden, by how we free those whose backs are against the wall. We can make heaven happy by how we treat children in the dawn of life, by how we treat the poor in the pit of life, and by how we treat seniors in the sunset of life.

The honor belongs to Edwin Clark and the glory belongs to God.

25

With Justice for All: Human Rights and Civil Rights at Home and Abroad

**Cambridge Union Society
Cambridge, England
December 2, 2013**

I want to thank Cambridge University for inviting me to speak to you this evening. It is always a joy and privilege for me to come to the United Kingdom. I have treasured memories of my earliest visits, marching with Bishop Trevor Huddleston against apartheid in Trafalgar Square in the early 1980s. Later I met with British prime minister Margaret Thatcher when I was on my way to South Africa to witness Nelson Mandela gaining his freedom from prison.

Now it is a distinct and prestigious opportunity to be able to engage and share with your students, faculty, and staff tonight at this prestigious, world-renowned educational institution, whose alumni have played such a huge role in the way the modern world sees itself.

I am honored to be here. I grew up in the segregated South, in Greenville, South Carolina, behind what I call the "cotton curtain." Somehow, some way, thanks to the grace of God, I was able to emerge from behind that curtain and those walls and barriers to be with you this evening.

I was recently in the Netherlands, Germany, and Belgium. What struck me is we live today in an emerging new Europe and a new Britain. It's far different from the one of your parents and the Winston Churchill generation. That Europe related to Jamaica and the Caribbean, India, China, Bangladesh, Nigeria, and South Africa as "colonies and colonized people," living under the sting of apartheid.

These former colonized people are now Britain's newest immigrants and newest citizens who have brought their cultures, languages, hopes, dreams, and interests to the United Kingdom. Your current generation now relates to Britain's newest residents as neighbors, classmates, business partners, members of parliament, and voting partners.

There are three million blacks and ethnic minorities in the United Kingdom today, growing to some eight million in the next decade, with 22 percent living in poverty. In large degree they are marginalized, and, as in the United States, they face structural inequalities in criminal justice, education, employment, housing, and health care. They are disproportionately at the bottom in nearly every social, economic, political, and educational category in the life of Britain.

These structural disparities are well documented by Equanomics UK. And formulating government policy to address them will be at the forefront of a racial justice manifesto that will be put before your parties and candidates running up to your national elections next year. As their population grows, so too will their voting and political power, and so too will their demand for equality and a level playing field.

So forging a new United Kingdom—one that is inclusive and sets a level playing field for its entire people—brings forth new challenges and opportunities.

Britain's new leaders of your generation are challenged to move away from living in isolation and governing in isolation. Now their opportunity is to commit to forging a multicultural, multiracial inclusive society, a one-big-tent Britain and Europe. The gaps between rich and poor must be closed, not widened.

Today we are free but not equal. Today we are caught in a global economic crisis. We have globalized capital, but we have not globalized human rights. We have not globalized workers' rights. We have not globalized rights for women, rights for children, and rights for environmental protections.

Our technological wizardry has outstripped our ethical high ground. We need instead to mesh new technology with timeless moral values. Like magic, capital today can move quickly, seek out poverty wages and slave labor, and leave behind devastated people, communities, and unfathomable pain. Finance circles the globe at the click of a button, and trillions in wealth can disappear or move offshore in moments. While we sleep at night, an invisible hand of the wealthy trades in the wealth that the people of the world have created.

Since the beginning of the Great Recession in 2007 the modern-day system of finance capital has collapsed. That system has failed. And it put in peril millions upon millions of everyday working people in the United States and around the world. We don't want to diminish the creativity of capital ingenuity and productivity, but neither do we want to diminish the significance of a strong public infrastructure and laws that make such ingenuity possible. Every crisis provides an opportunity. Now it is our time for a change moment to remake the world's financial systems. Now is our time to pass a "Robin Hood" tax on financial speculation—take back the money of the poor that the rich stole and return it to the poor. Now is our chance to globalize human rights and workers' rights, protect women and children, and save the global environment. Now is our chance to democratize capital and media. Too few people control too much wealth and information outlets, leveraging too much political influence for a healthy democratic outcome.

Democratic (small "d") government must play a stronger role, not a lesser role. We've seen the disastrous economic crisis resulting from that philosophy. Government must intervene to regulate and enforce needed checks and balances to curb unmitigated greed. It must intervene to protect the majority from the tyranny of the ruling economic and political minority.

As Dr. Martin Luther King Jr. argued, "government must use

its vast resources to wage an all-out world war against poverty." We must move toward freedom and equality from poverty and despair.

Eight million families and forty million Americans, or 13 percent of our population, live in poverty; fourteen million children under eighteen live in poverty. In 2008, forty-nine million people didn't have enough to eat, including seventeen million children.

In 2002, thirty-five million US citizens went hungry, a number that has increased by 40 percent since then. In the end, the Barack Obama administration and our nations—like each of us—will be judged by how we treat the least of these. Hemmed in by stunted hopes, circumscribed lives, and broken dreams, the "other America" that shocked President John F. Kennedy still exists.

Dr. King knew well the life and death impact of government policies; the upside-down priorities of immoral leadership. Dr. King understood that the Vietnam War was not just killing people overseas but killing people in our barrios and ghettoes back home. The war on Vietnam killed the war on poverty and ruined President Lyndon Johnson's Great Society legacy. Dr. King challenged us to understand: "Nonviolence is the answer to the crucial political and moral questions of our time—the need for man to overcome oppression and violence without resorting to violence and oppression."

Increasingly Western powers are investing more and more in the military industry with fewer and fewer returns. They're trying to kill the mosquitoes of fear and pain (the manifestation) and not clean out the swamp of poverty and rejection (the causes). We in the West react to the manifestation of terrorism but ignore the conditions that breed it. Remember what is done in one country has rippling effects around the globe.

The world is a rainbow of people. The United States and the United Kingdom are becoming more diverse with each passing year. Our younger generation in America is more tolerant, more diverse, and more exposed to the larger world than their elders. That's a good thing, and it showed in our last presidential elections of 2008 and 2012, where young people led the way in a change election that ushered in President Barack Obama.

Remember when President George W. Bush and Prime Minister Tony Blair got together a few years ago to decide to invade Iraq? That was a minority meeting. When the big financial institution heads get together in New York or London—that's a minority meeting too. The United States and the United Kingdom together represent only 5 percent of the world, one out of every twenty people. Yet as all of you know, half the world lives in Asia, with almost half of them in China.

Too many Americans do not realize—and perhaps too many Europeans as well do not yet appreciate—that most people in the world are black, brown, yellow, young, female, non-Christian, and don't speak English. And the formerly colonized peoples are now moving into the once all-one-ethnic-group societies. This is Europe's big challenge for the future and the United Kingdom's big opportunity to build a new nation, to choose inclusion. We must unlearn an earlier lesson we practiced too well—how to survive apart. We must learn a new lesson—how to live and prosper together, choosing inclusion and growth. A comprehensive policy of inclusion is the roadmap to a new England to serve the emerging diverse world.

We must find common ground. Common ground leads to coalition, to cooperation, to reconciliation and redemption, and to higher moral and economic ground. The challenge of this new world, so connected by technology, is yours to bear and yours to share. I want to say to you young people especially—keep reaching beyond your grasp, keep dreaming beyond your circumstances, keep dreaming of a new Europe. When young people move, the world changes.

Absent an active and vocal movement, we cannot make our hope for change a lasting and concrete reality. When twelve abolitionists met together two-and-a-quarter centuries ago in London to fight back against the profitable slave trade, few thought they would succeed. But they persisted, and the English antislavery advocate William Wilberforce prevailed, and the slave trade was soon ended. Dream of a new world.

When the suffragists chained themselves to the fences of the British prime minister's home a century ago, few thought that women would soon win the right to vote. But they did by putting their bodies on the line for justice. And now women's rights fuel change in all parts of the globe. Dream of a new freedom.

As Dr. King taught us, "The arc of the universe is long, but it bends toward justice." Dream of a new day and of a new way. Go forward by hope and never backward by fear. And in the end, faith will not disappoint.

Keep hope alive!

Concluding Thoughts

I've never really felt there was much difference between my speeches and sermons—different approaches to achieve the same thing: conveying the good news. You have to start with the *isness* of the situation, the context of people's lives. Otherwise, you can end up with pietistic entertainment. It doesn't move the needle of social structures; it doesn't change the conditions of people's lives. But if you start with the *isness* of the situation, the rightness of it, you bring a sense of justice, you look for the goodness of the mercy of God. And you can usually find some biblical reference to deal with our everyday situation, because the story of Jesus is really telling the same story.

That's why Christianity is especially meaningful for African Americans. It's the same experience. Baby Jesus—living under a death warrant. A life with limited options. His earthly parents take him to Egypt as an immigrant, and he became a refugee. He came back teaching a living gospel, like water from a well that never runs dry. It was all about the poor, the poor, feeding them, loving them, emancipating them, being kind to them. He was challenging Rome's structures of injustice and limited life options. And he preached the "acceptable year of the Lord." That was revolutionary. So many of my sermons are about the same thing: How do you find the acceptable year of the Lord? You have to begin with what's in the news and speak to that situation.

In 1968, after Dr. King died, we were going forward with the Poor People's Campaign in Washington, which he had started. The plight of the poor was his magnificent obsession. We set up tents between the Lincoln Memorial and the Washington Monument called "Resurrection City." Reverend Abernathy, Dr. King's partner and successor, asked me to be "mayor" of our camp. Conditions were pretty rough; people had nothing, and it rained every day we were there. We were trapped in the mud. Two of our sojourners died with hepatitis in the city. Our spirits were low. People had nothing to go on except for their souls and the will to dignity. Dr. King had been killed on April 4, 1968, and Robert Kennedy, who attended the funeral, was killed on June 6. The men that Dr. King had negotiated with at the White House were turning their backs on us. A sense of despair was in the wind.

Every morning I got on the back of a truck to give directions as to what our project was for the day. People were looking up at me. They had no money, no bus fare. I did not know what to say to them. I remembered reading a book by Howard Thurman, *Jesus and the Disinherited,* where he talks about what it means when your back is against the wall. You are reduced to an irreducible essence, naked against the world. But you are still somebody, you are still God's child. You matter.

And so I said to the people, "You still matter. *You are somebody.*" And I had them repeat those words: *"I am somebody."* And that became a refrain in so many talks and gatherings. It came out of talking to people whose backs were against the wall, people who had lost their sense of somebodiness.

"I may be poor, I may be unemployed, but I am somebody."

I've been all around the world, and it resonates as much as it did fifty years ago; all around, in every language, people struggle for a sense of somebodiness—marginalized people struggling to find some hope for oxygen, something that helps you to breathe. It never grows old.

And then in 1988, we got double digits in Iowa during my second run for the presidency; we started out strong. There was a heightened sense of anticipation. We won Michigan. We were doing very well. We did well in Wisconsin, and we moved very well in New York. But then we lost the New York primary, and some people were giving up. They didn't want to continue. They said that we could not win mathematically. And I said there are key people in Illinois, California, and around the country who are counting on us. We can't tell them that the campaign is over. You have to KEEP HOPE ALIVE. *KEEP HOPE ALIVE!* You can't give up. That's where that phrase came—from a dark moment in that campaign. We didn't win. But we never gave up.

What sustains my own hope? Faith is often defined as the substance of things hoped for and the evidence of things unseen. I have seen enough substantial changes in my lifetime, from being in the back of the bus to the front of the White House. There is progress that sustains my hope. My prayer life and the people God has sent into my life are cogenerational. Sometimes I inspire them, and they always inspire me. I've lived long enough to see rays of light, and I know the difference between the sunrise and a train coming at you. But it has all been a blessing. When it is really dark, a little light will do you.

The biblical parable of the sower says you sow seeds. Some hit the wind; they do not have a chance to germinate. Some seeds hit the rock and never have a chance. Some blossom in front of the sower, and some blossom in fertile soil. You never know what seed will blossom into a special genius, who may have the capacity to cure AIDS, cancer, or other diseases. A writer says, "Leaders sow seeds, and may never sit under the shade of the trees they planted." Now I've been around long enough to have planted seeds, and watch trees grow, and I have sat under the shade and watched them multiply. This is what happened. There was a tree that germinated—that seed germinated into a tree to become president.

I lived long enough to be a part of that night when Barack Obama was elected. I watched that tree grow. I watched my son, Jesse Jr., go to Congress; I saw that seed grow. There are those in the Congress today, House and Senate, mayors, legislators, and ministers who say they attended some high school rally or some demonstration where their seed was watered. Nothing is more gratifying. I sat under the tree, and I keep planting other trees. Thanks be to God to live long enough for doing that.

My strength was always my relationship with the people. When I traveled I stayed in people's homes instead of downtown hotels. Coal miners' homes. Meat cutters', housing projects, gang bangers' in LA. And when I was speaking I saw them. My refrain at the time was, "I understand." I knew who I was talking to—the woman, the coal miner, speaking to the *isness*. And I wasn't quoting Scripture. I was *scripturing*.

But I'd usually end up with Scripture. I used to say, *I know it's dark but the morning comes. . . . The Lord is my light and my salvation, who should I fear? . . . Job: Though you slay me yet will I trust you.*

The numerators are the issues that keep coming and changing. But you have to be grounded in the denominator. The numerators may be South Africa, Iran-Contra, Iraq, Libya, North Korea, Venezuela, the shooting down of children in the streets, which gave rise to the protests around Black Lives Matter. They vary. But your grounding, your worldview—peace and justice, the ethics of Jesus—doesn't change. The fundamental message remains: good news to the poor, healing the broken hearted, setting the captive free, the acceptable year of the Lord. That doesn't change much. That is the denominator. Jesus said, Love the Lord and love your neighbor as yourself. That doesn't change.

I'm old and I have Parkinson's, but once I was young. I went to jail with my classmates when I was nineteen, trying to use the public library, and now I'm seventy-seven. I have been around the world many times since then; I have experienced many of life's ups and downs, breakthroughs and failures, moments of rejoicing and deep-felt pain and sorrow. I identify with the words of the psalmist who writes, "I once was young, but now I am old. I have never seen the righteous forsaken, nor their seed beg for bread." After all these years, what remains for me is God is a source of mystery and wonder. Scripture holds up. The righteous are not forsaken. We've come a long way since slavery time. But we're not finished yet. Running for freedom is a long-distance race.[1]

Jesse L. Jackson Sr.
Chicago, May 28, 2019

Afterword

Keep Fighting

When I was fifteen years old, I attended the 1984 Democratic National Convention as a special guest of the Mississippi Democratic Party. It was, without exaggeration, an extraordinary experience. Ms. Dorothy Miles, a leader of the party in Jackson County, made it all happen. She watched me canvas neighborhoods in the brutal Mississippi heat and put up yard signs for candidates. She also saw that, in the same year of the convention, I had been elected the first black youth governor in the Mississippi YMCA Youth Legislature. Many wondered, perhaps naïvely given what has happened since, if the young people of the state foreshadowed what was possible. Ms. Miles believed a trip to San Francisco would deepen my political passions and give me an opportunity to see, up close, national politics at work. She was right. With a few phone calls, I had my credentials, and I was on a plane, alone, to California.

The Mississippi delegation drew one of the worst hotels available to delegates. We were right on the edge of the Tenderloin district, on the southern slope of Nob Hill. For a Catholic country boy from the Gulf Coast, I had never seen anything like what I saw. And I saw everything. Secrets I will take to my grave. We had the best seats in the convention hall. I watched as Mario Cuomo delivered his famous "Tale of Two Cities" speech. I witnessed up close the intense battles raging within the convention as the established black political class and white Democratic power brokers tried desperately to beat back the insurgent campaign of Rev. Jesse Jackson.

195

Reverend Jackson's historic presidential run in 1984 shook the foundations of the party. He campaigned for deep cuts in defense spending, for jobs, health care, public housing, for protecting the environment, policies to benefit both rural and urban America, and for a politics less concerned about the well-being of the rich and more focused on the conditions of the most vulnerable among us. His appeal cut across traditional divides as a "rainbow coalition" offered a different vision of the country. I watched as Julian Bond, Andrew Young, and Coretta Scott King urged the Jackson delegates to support Walter Mondale. I stood, with my mouth agape, as they booed Mrs. King. In some ways, and perhaps it was the last gasp of a dying era, Rev. Jackson brought the energy of the civil rights movement into the electoral process; and the black political elites of the Democratic Party were expected to fall in line.

I will never forget Rev. Jackson's speech. As a young, black teenager from the Deep South, he expanded my imagination of what was possible. Honestly, I had never seen anything or heard anyone like him (at least, in the flesh). Whatever Barack Obama's campaign inspired in this generation, I am confident I felt it on the night of July 18, 1984. One way to put it would be that what Selma was to Rev. Jackson, this moment—against the backdrop of Ronald Reagan—was to me. Something powerfully transformative happened when Rev. Jackson stepped to the podium. Pipe dreams and adolescent illusions about what was possible in this country fell to the side as the reality of Jackson's powerful challenge to the status quo flooded the convention hall. His opening lines revealed the underlying theology of his public witness—a theology evidenced in these pages.

> Tonight we come together bound by our faith in a mighty God, with genuine respect and love for our country, and inheriting the legacy of a great party, the Democratic Party, which is the best hope for redirecting our nation on a more humane, just, and peaceful course.
>
> This is not a perfect party. We are not a perfect people. Yet, we are called to a perfect mission. Our mission: to feed the

hungry; to clothe the naked; to house the homeless; to teach the illiterate; to provide jobs for the jobless; and to choose the human race over the nuclear race.

I clung to every word. He laid bare a vision and a challenge to the party and to the country that fundamentally rejected the callous policies of Reagan and modern conservatism. It was a vision rooted in his Christian commitment to exemplify the ministry and sacrifice of Jesus in our contemporary living.

Reverend Jackson ended his speech like a good Baptist preacher. I vaguely remember being carried away by it all. What I remember most, and time hasn't diminished the memory at all, was a feeling of being charged to do more and to be better.

Our time has come. Our time has come. Suffering breeds character. Character breeds faith. In the end, faith will not disappoint.

Our time has come. Our faith, hope, and dreams will prevail. Our time has come. Weeping has endured for nights, but now joy cometh in the morning.

Our time has come. No grave can hold our body down. Our time has come. No lie can live forever.

Our time has come. We must leave racial battleground and come to economic common ground and moral higher ground. America, our time has come. We come from disgrace to amazing grace.

Our time has come. Give me your tired, give me your poor, your huddled masses who yearn to breathe free and come November, there will be a change because our time has come.

Reverend Jackson bookended his convention speech with a political theology that informed his work since the early days of Operation Breadbasket. His rhetoric and style contained the blue note of slavery and segregation, the difficulty and promise of migration, and the resilient hope of a people who faced ongoing betrayal by country. Reverend Jackson brought to the convention floor *our* tradition in the service, as it has been before, of saving the nation. No theological abstractions were necessary. Just an affirmation of the personality and dignity of every human being no matter their color, gender, sexual orientation, or zip code in pursuit of a more just world.

I remember walking into an elevator. I don't recall where or what was the context. I was alone, or I think I was alone (time is ruthless with details), and I had my head down. Somewhat overwhelmed by it all, I was in my own little world thinking about what I had seen and experienced. My hometown of Moss Point seemed so small now. I knew I would never be the same. The elevator stopped. The doors opened. I looked up, and in walked Rev. Jackson with his entourage. He towered above me, and I kept staring endlessly upward. He was so tall. Reverend Jackson smiled, shook my hand firmly, and asked where I was from. I don't remember much of what was said after that except his final words as he walked out of the elevator. "Keep studying and keep fighting."

These sermons and speeches demonstrate that Rev. Jackson has never stopped fighting. He has had a long, public life, full of peaks and valleys—he would never claim to be perfect or without sin—but his abiding faith in the capacity of ordinary people to transform the world has fortified his spirit to continue to fight on behalf of the least of these. Reverend Jackson's political theology is rooted in a fundamental understanding of the life of Jesus and in the example of Dr. King. It is a social gospel attuned to the personality of each individual (I am somebody!) and carried forward by stories that bring the good news down to earth in the lived experiences of people and in pursuit of justice.

As the first collection of Rev. Jackson's sermons and speeches, I hope this book will spark renewed interest in his public witness and the thinking that shapes it. Students and scholars now have a resource to begin the examination of how his particular theological views informed and shaped his politics. How does he think about love? What is the relationship between his view of love and justice? What are his theological resources? And how might we understand the ongoing work of translation that is his rhetorical practice. Students and scholars can also begin to tackle the contradictions in his thinking and practice, and map the differences between his views and approach and those of Dr. King. Such work reaches beyond the matter of biography; it requires more than a description of a particular political moment. With Rev. Jackson's words in hand we can now begin to unpack his political and religious thought (understanding always that both are never separable from his praxis).

In the end, *Keeping Hope Alive* demonstrates how much of what Rev. Jackson has said and done blazed a path for us today. His words still offer a pathway for the country to be otherwise, especially in these dark times when democracy, battered and bruised, cowers in the corner. A resiliency and grit leaps from every page. His never-ending faith (in himself, in us, and in God) fuels a progressive vision. And in rereading his words, I am reminded of what he told me when I was a just fifteen-year-old boy: "Keep fighting!" That fight back, more than anything else, will keep hope alive.

Eddie S. Glaude Jr.
James S. McDonnell Distinguished
University Professor
Chair, Department of
African American Studies
Princeton University

Notes

1. *The Message of Easter*

1. The Rainbow PUSH Coalition is the product of a social justice movement that grew out of the Southern Christian Leadership Conference's (SCLC) Operation Breadbasket. Founded by Rev. Dr. Martin Luther King Jr., Operation Breadbasket sought to combine theology and social justice and to effect progressive economic, educational, and social policy in America. In 1966 Dr. King appointed Jesse L. Jackson Sr. to serve as the first director of Operation Breadbasket in Chicago, Illinois. The Rainbow PUSH Coalition is the result of a merger between Operation PUSH and the National Rainbow Coalition. Established in 1971 by Rev. Jackson, PUSH (People United to Save Humanity; later changed from "Save" to "Serve") was an organization dedicated to improving the economic conditions of black communities across the United States.

2. In Matthew 26:36–39, it reads: "Then cometh Jesus with them unto a place called Gethsemane, and saith unto the disciples, Sit ye here, while I go and pray yonder. And he took with him Peter and the two sons of Zebedee, and began to be sorrowful and very heavy. Then saith he unto them, My soul is exceeding sorrowful, even unto death: tarry ye here, and watch with me. And he went a little further, and fell on his face, and prayed, saying, O my Father, if it be possible, let this cup pass from me: nevertheless not as I will, but as thou wilt" (King James Version).

3. Frederick Douglass, "West India Emancipation, Speech Delivered at Canandaigua, New York, August 4, 1857," in *The Life and Writings of Frederick Douglass, Volume 2: Pre-Civil War Decade*, ed. Philip S. Foner (4 vols.; New York: International Publishers, 1950), 437.

4. Emmett Louis Till (1941–1955) was a fourteen-year-old black boy from Chicago who was spending the summer with family members in Mississippi. One day, maybe showing off to his Mississippi cousins, Emmett went into a white store and, when he was about to leave, he said to a white woman there, "Bye baby." In retaliation that woman's husband and brother-in-law abducted Emmett Till later that night, savagely tor-

tured him, shot him through the head, and tossed his body in the Tallahatchie River. Some say that the heinous execution of this young African American boy was an event that inspired the protest of Rosa Parks, the Montgomery bus boycott that ensued, and the onset of the modern civil rights movement. See Mamie Till-Mobley and Christopher Benson, *Death of Innocence: The Story of the Hate Crime That Changed America* (New York: World/Ballantine, 2004).

5. The invasion of Iraq on March 19, 2003, one month before this sermon was delivered, was preceded by an overwhelming bombing campaign entitled "Shock and Awe."

6. Isaiah 2:4 (King James Version): "And he shall judge among the nations, and shall rebuke many people: and they shall beat their swords into plowshares, and their spears into pruning hooks: nation shall not lift up sword against nation, neither shall they learn war anymore."

7. The annual meeting of the Organization of American Historians was held in Memphis, Tennessee, April 3–6, 2003. To mark the thirty-fifth anniversary of the assassination of the Rev. Dr. Martin Luther King Jr., conference participants staged a symbolic march from the LeMoyne-Owen College to Mason Temple, the location of Dr. King's last speech, which was delivered during the evening of April 3, 1968. The next day, Dr. King was murdered while standing on the balcony of the Lorraine Motel.

8. The two major campaigns of Dr. King, right before his assassination, were supporting black garbage workers in Memphis, Tennessee, and building a new coalition of red, yellow, white, brown, and black poor people to set up tents in the spring of 1968 in Washington, DC. The plan was to have the poor stay in the nation's capital until they were heard by the nation's leaders. King stated the demands as jobs, unemployment insurance, education for poor adults and children, and a fair minimum wage.

2. *The Moral Center*

1. See Martin Luther King Jr., "A Time to Break Silence," in *A Testament of Hope: The Essential Writings of Martin Luther King, Jr.*, ed. James M. Washington (San Francisco: Harper & Row, 1986), 231–44. For more about that fateful speech, see Vincent Harding, *Martin Luther King: The Inconvenient Hero* (Maryknoll, NY: Orbis Books, 1996).

2. Dr. King used this refrain in many sermons and speeches. For example, see "It's a Dark Day in Our Nation," preached at Ebenezer Baptist Church, Atlanta, Georgia, April 30, 1967.

3. At his death, Dr. King focused on two movements: supporting the black working-class garbage workers' movement in Memphis, Tennessee, and organizing a massive poor people's campaign to march on Washington in the spring of 1968. See also Chapter 1, note 8.

4. Walter Fauntroy was the director of the Washington, DC, bureau of the Southern Christian Leadership Conference, the national civil rights organization headed by Dr. King.

5. On the movement to abolish slavery (roughly 1619 to 1865), see John Bright, *Frederick Douglass: Prophet of Freedom* (New York: Simon & Schuster, 2018); W. E. B. Du Bois, *The Suppression of the African Slave Trade to the United States of America 1638–1870* (Amazon Digital Services).

In July 1848, the women's suffrage movement began at the Seneca Falls Convention (the first women's rights convention held in Seneca, New York), where women put forth the first formal demand for women's right to vote. The Bread and Roses strike is the name of the successful January to March 1912 textile workers' strike in Lawrence, Massachusetts. Bread stood for fair wages, and roses meant dignified working conditions. The December 1936–February 1937 auto workers' strike in Flint, Michigan, against General Motors Corporation helped the United Auto Workers to become a national union.

Cesar Chavez (1937–1993), a Mexican American farm worker who became a national civil rights and labor leader, formed, with Dolores Huerta, the National Farm Workers Association, which became the United Farm Workers union. The successful December 1955 Montgomery bus boycott was led by Dr. King to protest segregated sitting on city public buses in Montgomery, Alabama. The boycott began December 1, 1955, when Mrs. Rosa Parks refused to give her bus seat to a white man, and ended December 20, 1956, with the US Supreme Court's decision that Alabama's bus segregation laws were unconstitutional. See Martin Luther King Jr., *Stride Toward Freedom: The Montgomery Story* (New York: HarperCollins, 1987).

The 1965 March from Selma, Alabama, to Montgomery, Alabama, eventually led to the 1965 passage of the Voting Rights Act. The march and Dr. Martin Luther King Jr.'s 1963 letter, written while incarcerated in a Birmingham, Alabama, jail, are major markers in the 1950s and 1960s civil rights movement. At 1:20 a.m., Saturday morning, June 28, 1969, the New York City police raided the Stonewall Inn in Manhattan, a popular gay bar. The gay community fought back, and this rebellion signals the beginning of a national gay liberation movement.

The August 28, 1963, March on Washington, of 250,000 to 300,000 people at the Lincoln Memorial, focused on jobs and freedom. The civil rights Freedom Riders were blacks and whites riding together on interstate buses in the Southern United States to protest segregation on interstate transportation. Police and white vigilante groups reacted by beating peaceful demonstrators with iron pipes, baseball bats, and burning busses, and arresting the integrated riders. In certain cases Ku Klux Klan members had just come from a church service and worked with local police to beat riders to near unconsciousness. Ten weeks in June of 1964 were called Freedom Summer, or the Mississippi Summer Project, and witnessed over one thousand student volunteers going around and attempting to register blacks to vote. Official police along with the Ku Klux Klan and other white vigilante groups beat and terrorized hundreds of activists. They murdered at least three young voter registration volunteers.

The Students for a Democratic Society (SDS) was a radical, predominantly white, student group that issued a major 1962 statement calling on participatory democracy and nonviolent civil disobedience. The statement was issued from Port Huron, Michigan. Written at their national convention, this statement was a major expression of vision and a turning point in the white New Left (particularly student) movement.

Regarding the Vietnam Moratorium, on October 15, 1969, over two million citizens across the United States participated in a variety of demonstrations protesting the US invasion, bombing, and occupation of Vietnam. Similarly, particularly in the 1980s, hundreds of thousands of US citizens demonstrated to protest the US support of apartheid.

6. In 1963, Cassius Clay (later Muhammad Ali) fought British boxer Henry Cooper. Cooper hit Clay with a left hook at the end of the fourth round. On his way to the floor, Clay caught the ropes. In round five, Clay hit Cooper so hard that a severe cut appeared under his right eye, and the referee had to stop the fight and declare Clay the winner. In the postfight interview, Clay responded to the question, "What does it feel like to be knocked down?" with his own now famous words: "The ground is no place for a champion."

7. Premier of the Peoples Republic of China, Zhou Enlai was meeting with President Richard Nixon in China, February 1972. Nixon was the first US president to visit China since its 1949 revolution. During their talks, Nixon asked Zhou what he thought about the implications of the French Revolution on Western culture. Zhou replied, "Too early to tell."

8. This statement is from Lord Acton (Sir John Dalberg-Acton;

1834–1902), who was an English Catholic historian, writer, and politician. "Power tends to corrupt and absolute power corrupts absolutely."

9. Luke 10:29–37. Jesus tells the story about who is our true neighbor. A man is beaten badly and left on the Jericho road. A priest and a Levite pass him by, but a Samaritan stranger helps and pays for a place to stay.

10. Thomas Paine was born in England and wrote two important works that impacted the thinking and passion of the 1776 American Revolution against King George in England. His *Common Sense* (1776) pamphlet was the most widely read popular publication in US history, and it gave clear reasons why the thirteen colonies should fight for independence against Britain. And his *American Crisis* (1776–1783) pamphlets were ongoing popular explanations supporting the American Revolution. His first pamphlet (1776) in the series contained the famous words, "These are the times that try men's souls."

3. Beauty from the Ashes

1. Harvey Fireside, *Separate and Unequal: Homer Plessy and the Supreme Court Decision That Legalized Racism* (New York: Carroll & Graf, 2003); Lawrence Goldstone, *Inherently Unequal: The Betrayal of Equal Rights by the Supreme Court, 1865–1903* (New York: Walker & Company, 2011). The Thirteenth Amendment to the US Constitution abolished slavery. The Fourteenth gave equal protection under the law to all citizens. The 1875 Civil Rights Act granted full and equal enjoyment to all public accommodations. *Plessy v. Ferguson,* which upheld the constitutionality of racial segregation, gutted the Fourteenth Amendment and overturned the 1875 Civil Rights Act.

2. On March 21, 1960, black South Africans decided to protest the apartheid law that made them carry identity passbooks in their own country. Demonstrators refused to carry passbooks. In response, the white South African police shot sixty-nine unarmed men, women, and children. Because the deaths took place in the Sharpeville township, this day is known as the Sharpeville Massacre; and, since 1994, it is commemorated as Human Rights Day. News spread of the killings, and black South Africans carried out nationwide demonstrations. Countries around the world condemned the massacre, and the United Nations also condemned the deadly attack.

3. "Coloured" was the South African designation for persons of mixed race.

4. Regina Mundi (Queen of the World) is the largest Roman Catholic church in South Africa. Located in Soweto, the densest black South African urban area (located in Johannesburg), it served as a major meeting place for students and adults who fought against apartheid. At one point, white policeman entered and shot up the church. Crossroads is a black South African township near Cape Town. It, too, has a long history of being famous in its opposition to apartheid and apartheid's infamous forced resettlement of black South Africans from their indigenous lands.

5. From 1948, when the Afrikaner Nationalist Party came to power and universalized the practice of apartheid nationwide, until the first democratic election in the history of South Africa in 1994 (one that saw the presidential election of Nelson Mandela), a secret society ran South Africa. It was called the Afrikaner Broederbond (Afrikaner Brotherhood). White male Afrikaners of the white Dutch Reformed Church were members. They influenced and controlled every aspect of apartheid in South Africa, including the church, government, gold and diamond industries, and other pillars of civil society. See Ivor Wilkins and Hans Strydom, *The Super-Afrikaners: Inside the Afrikaner Broederbond* (1st ed.; Johannesburg: Jonathan Ball, 1978).

6. Soweto (a large black township in Johannesburg) is one of the major markers in the history of the anti-apartheid movement for democracy. On June 16, 1976, students in Soweto demonstrated and marched against the white government's introduction of Afrikaans as the official language to be used by South African students. Afrikaans symbolized concentrated apartheid at its worse because Afrikaans was the official language of the Afrikaners. In response to student protest, the government murdered, in some estimates, up to seven hundred students. Black South Africans across the country demonstrated in solidarity with Soweto. South Africa entered a deeper crisis, and the international community increasingly condemned white apartheid South Africa. The government became even more isolated globally.

7. Allan A. Boesak is an ordained Dutch Reformed clergyman with a PhD in systematic theology. With political organizations banned by the white apartheid government (and so folks were in exile, in jail, underground, or murdered), two religious figures were the public face of resistance to apartheid: Archbishop Desmond Tutu and Allan A. Boesak, whose church, under apartheid, was located in Cape Town.

8. See Walter Rodney, *How Europe Underdeveloped Africa* (Baltimore, MD: Black Classic Press, 2011).

4. *Faith without Works Is Dead*

1. Leon H. Sullivan (1922–2001) was a major Baptist pastor in Philadelphia, civil rights activist, and advocate for jobs and economic development for black Americans. When white corporations refused to honor Sullivan's request to interview more black job applicants, he led major boycotts in Philadelphia. As a result, thousands of jobs were opened up for African Americans. "Don't buy where you don't work" became an effective strategy for getting the attention of corporate America. In addition to creating new jobs, he also trained blacks for jobs and created new black businesses. Dr. King asked him to help with boycotts in other cities. He was also a national leader organizing American corporations to boycott South Africa.

2. In 1962, the Southern Christian Leadership Conference launched Operation Breadbasket in Atlanta, Georgia, to focus on the economic plight of blacks across the United States. One of the initial points was that black people should not patronize businesses that did not hire them. In 1966, I became head of the Chicago chapter of Operation Breadbasket. In 1967, I became the national director.

3. For important works on the history of America and African Americans, see John Hope Franklin and Alfred A. Moss, *From Slavery to Freedom: A History of African Americans* (8th ed.; New York: McGraw-Hill, 2000); Manning Marable and Leith Mullings, eds., *Let Nobody Turn Us Around: An African American Anthology* (Lanham, MD: Rowman & Littlefield, 2009); and Robin D. G. Kelley and Earl Lewis, eds., *To Make Our World Anew: A History of African Americans* (New York: Oxford University Press, 2000).

4. President Abraham Lincoln signed the Emancipation Proclamation on January 1, 1863, freeing all blacks who were enslaved in the Confederate states that had seceded from the United States. However, if a state remained part of the United States, it could keep blacks enslaved. The Civil War officially ended in 1865. On February 3, 1870, Congress ratified the Fifteenth Amendment to the US Constitution. From 1867 to 1868, Congress passed four reconstruction acts detailing how the former Confederate states could reenter the union of the United States: blacks were allowed to vote and hold office and property, the major former Confederate leaders were denied the right to vote and the right to hold office, and the federal government would station troops in the South to enable full political, economic, and social participation of the formerly enslaved population. In 1877, Reconstruction ended, and the Confederates came

back to power. See W. E. B. Du Bois, *Black Reconstruction in America: 1860–1880* (New York: Free Press, 1999).

5. The Great Global Recession of 2007 and onward was created mainly by US banks that gave out housing loans to people who were not fully qualified. These risky loans were bundled and sold on the global market. It was a house of cards, and the financial system eventually crashed, taking down banks, closing businesses, causing massive foreclosures and unemployment.

5. Wrestling with the Living Word

1. Reverend Randolph Bracy Jr. and his wife, Dr. LaVon Wright Bracy, were founders of the New Covenant Baptist Church of Orlando.

2. Michelle Alexander, *The New Jim Crow: Mass Incarceration in the Age of Colorblindness* (New York: New Press, 2012).

3. On the civil rights struggle in Selma, see Sheyann Webb-Christburg et al., *Selma, Lord, Selma: Girlhood Memories of the Civil Rights Days* (Tuscaloosa, AL: University of Alabama Press, 1997), and David J. Garrow, *Protest at Selma: Martin Luther King, Jr., and the Voting Rights Act of 1965* (New Haven, CT: Yale University Press, 1980).

4. Medgar Evers was a major leader in the National Association for the Advancement of Colored People in Mississippi. He was assassinated by a white man (a member of the white supremacist White Citizens Council) while exiting his car in the driveway of his home on June 12, 1963. Fannie Lou Hamer was a major grass-roots organizer and leader of the Mississippi Freedom Democratic Party. This party was democratically elected by open votes, and it went to the 1964 Democratic Party National Convention in New Jersey where it asked President Lyndon Johnson to recognize them as the true representatives of the people of Mississippi. The MFDP was considered illegal, and the legal delegation from the state was an all-white male delegation.

James Chaney, Andrew Goodman, and Michael Schwerner were three young civil rights workers killed by the local sheriff's office, the local police, and the Ku Klux Klan in Neshoba County, Mississippi, June 21–22, 1964.

6. My Father's Church

1. The Front Line States comprised an organization of Angola, Botswana, Lesotho, Mozambique, Swaziland, Tanzania, Zambia, and,

from 1980, Zimbabwe. They initially came together in 1970 and were resolute in their opposition to apartheid South Africa, in support of the South African liberation groups, and in the fostering of democracy in the new postapartheid South Africa.

2. Oliver R. Tambo (1917–1993) is the second most recognized leader, after Nelson Mandela, of the African National Congress of the anti-apartheid generation. In 1943, Tambo, Walter Sisulu, and Mandela were the founding members of the African National Congress Youth League.

3. Pastor Robert Kelley, a native of Washington, DC, is the founding pastor (in the year 2000) of My Father's House Christian Fellowship Church in Johannesburg, South Africa. Pastor Kelley's leadership has built the church up to over 1,200 members representing over fourteen nationalities throughout the African continent.

4. Frank Chikane (b. 1951), the son of a preacher and ordained in the Apostolic Faith Mission of South Africa, served as general secretary of the South African Council of Churches. Johnny Mfanafuthi Makatini (1932–1988) was a member of the African National Congress Executive Committee and head of the ANC Mission to the United Nations.

5. Chris Hani (1942–1993) was a leader in the South African Communist Party and the military wing of the African National Congress— Umkhonto we Sizwe. One day, when he was stepping out of his car, he was assassinated by a white pro-apartheid man. Steve Biko (1942–1977) is the recognized founder of the Black Consciousness Movement in South Africa. While in custody, he was assassinated by the South African police.

6. Winnie Mandela (b. 1936), the wife of Nelson Mandela before their divorce in 1996, was an anti-apartheid leader who suffered harassment, imprisonment, torture, and house arrest. She headed the African National Congress Women's League and is on the National Executive Committee of the ANC.

7. Mandela forgave his jail guards on Robben Island for holding him in prison all of those years. He thus helped them to be free from the pain of the guilt they had carried. Instead of revenge, Mandela offered them reconciliation.

7. *The Rainbow Nation*

1. The text reprinted here has been edited for length, omitting passages dealing with economic and political issues of the day. The full text is available online.

2. The Simpson–Mazzoli Act, passed in 1986 and signed into law by President Ronald Reagan, made it a crime to knowingly employ illegal immigrants.

8. *Common Ground*

1. Aaron Henry (1922–1997) was head of the Mississippi branch of the NAACP. With Fannie Lou Hamer, he was one of the founders of the Mississippi Freedom Democratic Party delegation that sought to be recognized and seated at the 1964 Democratic Party Convention in Atlantic City, New Jersey. See Chapter 11, note 1.

9. *From Slavery to Freedom: Leveling the Playing Field*

1. From 1441, when Portuguese sailors brought a group of Africans, as slaves, back to the royalty of Portugal, until the abolition of slavery in Brazil in 1888, one hundred million Africans were impacted. For the relationship between the systematic development of Europe and the United States and the corresponding intentional underdevelopment of Africa and black Americans, see Walter Rodney, *How Europe Underdeveloped Africa* (Baltimore, MD: Black Classic Press, 2011); Eric Williams, *Capitalism and Slavery* (Chapel Hill, NC: University of North Carolina Press, 1994); and Manning Marable, *How Capitalism Underdeveloped Black America: Problems in Race, Political Economy, and Society* (Cambridge, MA: Beacon Press, 1999).

2. President Bush and his vice president, Dick Cheney, claimed that Iraq's president Saddam Hussein had weapons of mass destruction and was connected to al-Qaeda's September 11th attack. These two false pretenses were used by the president and his vice president to invade Iraq in order for American corporations to have access to Iraq's oil.

3. The G8 consists of France, Italy, Germany, Japan, Canada, England, the United States, and Russia. They met in Alberta, Canada, June 26–27, 2012. (In 2014 Russia was suspended from the group.)

4. In the United States in 2007, the top 20 percent of the population monopolized 88 percent of the nation's wealth; the bottom 80 percent of the citizens owned only 12 percent.

5. These four major corporations hid the level of their debt, avoided taxes, went out of business, and cost shareholders billions of dollars, while the executives of each of the four made hundreds of millions of dollars.

6. Passed by the US Congress and becoming law on June 23, 1972,

Title IX of the 1972 Education Amendments protects against sex discrimination in educational institutions that receive federal financial assistance.

7 The 2000 census listed 96.8 percent of East Los Angeles as being brown, Latino, or Hispanic peoples.

8. Redlining exists when realtors and mortgage-lending institutions steer potential black home buyers away from white neighborhoods and into more segregated and depressed-home-valued communities. By segregating whites into better, all-white areas, the wealth from these more highly appreciated homes will be passed on to white children and grandchildren. Redlining blacks means black parents possess negligible wealth or lack wealth to pass to their future generations. Home ownership and stocks represent two of the main ways American families accumulate wealth for their future family line.

10. *Beating Swords into Plowshares*

1. When I was a candidate for president of the United States, I flew to Syria in December 1983 and was able to free US Navy Lt. Robert O. Goodman, whose plane had been shot down.

2. During his incarceration, Mandela was so kind to one of his Afrikaner jailers that he called Mandela his father. After he became president of South Africa, Mandela made another of his former Afrikaner jailers the head of his security detail.

3. See Martin Luther King Jr., "A Time to Break Silence," in *A Testament of Hope: The Essential Writings of Martin Luther King, Jr.*, ed. James M. Washington (San Francisco: Harper & Row, 1986), 231–44.

11. *The Challenge to Build a More Perfect Union*

1. In 1964, the official Mississippi delegation to the 1964 Democratic National Convention was legally comprised of all white males. It was legal in Mississippi to keep black citizens out. In contrast, local black organizers (of the Mississippi Freedom Democratic Party) held an open democratic election where an alternative delegation was sent to the DNC. Both the legal white male and the illegal democratic delegation claimed they represented the people of Mississippi. Fannie Lou Hamer was a leader of the Mississippi Freedom Democratic Party at the convention, and she spoke on their behalf.

2. Ahmed Chalabi was an exiled Iraqi, an anti–Saddam Hussein politician who fed false information about Iraqi weapons to the Bush administration—false information that the president took incorrectly as

evidence for invading Iraq in March 2003. Hans Blix was the head of the UN Monitoring, Verification and Inspection Commission that found no weapons of mass destruction (WMDs) in Iraq.

12. *Globalization: The Promise and the Peril*

1. For a couple of perspectives on the subprime schemes leading to the 2007 Great Recession, see Robert J. Schiller, *The Subprime Solution: How Today's Global Financial Crisis Happened and What to Do about It* (Princeton, NJ: Princeton University Press, 2008); and Paula Chakravartty, ed. *Race, Empire, and the Crisis of the Subprime* (Special Issue of *American Quarterly*) (Baltimore, MD: Johns Hopkins University Press, 2013).

2. In April 1986 a catastrophic accident occurred at the nuclear power plant in Chernobyl in northern Soviet Ukraine. Radioactive contamination spread widely and forced the establishment of a 20-mile "exclusion zone" around the plant.

15. *The Journey of Our Ancestors*

1. The African Renaissance Monument, the largest statue in Africa, was unveiled outside Dakar, Senegal, on April 3, 2010. In the words of President Abdoulaye Wade, who initiated the project, the monument "brings to life our common destiny. Africa has arrived in the twenty-first century standing tall and more ready than ever to take its destiny into its hands. . . . This monument does not belong to Senegal. It belongs to the African people wherever we are."

16. *Speaking Truth to Power*

1. Christian Aid is the official organization of antipoverty and pro-relief and development for forty-one English and Irish churches. It covers Africa, Asia, the Caribbean, and Latin America. Its slogan is: We Believe in Life before Death.

2. "Bankster" refers to how banks acted as gangsters when they carried out predatory lending to many blacks, single women, workers, and poor people who received mortgage loans with very high interest rates. When the vulnerable couldn't pay mortgage loans, they stopped paying and forced banks to retake the homes. With no income from bad housing loans, banks did not have money to pay the interest on the packaged mortgage debt they sold around the world. A domino effect led to the collapse of global financial giants.

17. *Dr. King in Today's America*

1. On January 8, 2011, while standing in front of a supermarket greeting constituents in Tucson, Arizona, Gabrielle Giffords (congresswoman from Arizona), was shot in the head. Thirteen others were injured, and six others were killed, including a federal judge.

21. *Tribute to Nelson Mandela*

1. This event was part of the worldwide celebration of the ninety-fifth birthday of Nelson Mandela, born July 18, 1918. He died later that year, on December 5, 2013.

Concluding Thoughts

1. These reflections were drawn from a recorded conversation between Rev. Jackson and Robert Ellsberg and Grace Ji-Sun Kim at PUSH headquarters in Chicago, May 28, 2019.